THE
INNE...

for our children
and their children
and their children's children . . .

ALSO BY JOHN-FRANCIS PHIPPS

THE POLITICS OF
INNER EXPERIENCE

DYNAMICS OF A
GREEN SPIRITUALITY

John-Francis Phipps

First published in 1990 by
Green Print
an imprint of The Merlin Press
10 Malden Road, London NW5 3HR

ISBN 1 85425 025 6

1 2 3 4 5 6 7 8 9 10 :: 99 98 97 96 95 94 93 92 91 90

Phototypeset by Input Typesetting Ltd, London

Printed in England by Biddles Ltd., Guildford, Surrey
on recycled paper

ACKNOWLEDGEMENTS

I am especially grateful to Glenn Storhaug for having invited me to facilitate a discussion on 'Liberation of the Sublime' in Hereford in February 1987. This spurred me on to write this book.

Over the years Christopher Cornford has given me invaluable support and encouragement and I am grateful to him for providing the foreword. Sally Jenkinson has been most generous with her time and has also given invaluable advice. Warm thanks are also due to Victor, Edmund and Thomas de Waal; to Thomas Daffern; and to Ralph Maliphant, who helped me to overcome my resistance to the world of word-processors. I have also received much useful advice and constructive criticism from Jon Carpenter, editor at Green Print.

J-F.P.

Today we have entered an era when progress will be shaped by universal human interests. The awareness of this dictates that world politics, too, should be guided by the primacy of universal human values.

Mikhail Gorbachev
Address to the UN General Assembly
7th December, 1988

We are living between a death and a difficult birth.

Samuel Beckett

CONTENTS

FOREWORD

We live at a time when, as any reasonably thoughtful person can see, just about everything has gone appallingly wrong. Even if our species manages to avoid destroying itself and most other living creatures in a nuclear holocaust, we may well wreck our planetary life-support system only a little less abruptly by pollution, deforestation, climatic changes, nuclear accidents and other man-made disasters, nearly all of them the result of 'wealth-creating' activities on the part of the ruling elites of the so-called 'advanced' countries.

Can we save ourselves? Can we save the planet? It doesn't seem likely unless we can first understand why we have become so insanely destructive in the name of such shibboleths as 'defence', 'progress', 'development', 'technology', 'economic growth' and 'prosperity'. In this short and pithy treatise John-Francis Phipps offers a diagnosis that I find as deep-delving, as comprehensive and as convincing as any I have so far come across. Of necessity a certain amount of his critique of 'advanced' civilization will be familiar to readers who have come into contact with the counter-culture, especially with its environmentalist, anti-nuclear and feminist wings. But he adds syntheses and hypotheses of his own, the most important of which – and also the most difficult – are concerned with the philosophy of time. This he has been studying and pondering for many years: it was the theme of his 1982 pamphlet *Time and the Bomb*. Anthropologists tell us that pre-literate cultures have a radically different concept of time from our own. Western science has reduced it to a linear parameter, without any 'vertical' dimension like that embodied in the Dream Time of the Australian aboriginals, in the light of which the earth is sacred and could never be raped, pillaged and devastated as it is under the influence of our own secular and reductionist schema. We feel that something is missing but we don't know what.

To my mind, John-Francis Phipps *does* know, and tells us with simplicity and candour. Yet for all its directness this is not an easy text to absorb, the issues being so vast, so momentous and so complex in their interconnections. Moreover the author frequently seems to plunge us into the middle of a topic – say psycho-biological theories of aggression, or American fundamentalism – without the kind of lead-in which BBC-style expositions have led us to expect. To put the same point differently, he pays us the compliment of assuming that we can keep up with the leaps of his own agile mind. I suspect that in the long run this is an advantage: after a pause for digestion we are likely to want to go through it again. More will come through at each reading.

Above all what is enjoined here – as it was by the life and work of the great precursor William Blake – is that we should *both* apprehend the world mystically *and* try to save it by political activism of a new kind. Neither of these commitments will much avail without the other.

Christopher Cornford

INTRODUCTION

It is impossible to say exactly when I started to write this book. The last word was written in the unconscious long before I sat down and wrote the first. Many drafts were written over the course of several years, but even they only represent a fraction of the unconscious work (for which authors unfortunately do not get paid).

In terms of conventional chronology, I have been working on the general theme of Only Connect for at least twenty-five years. My belief in the need for some kind of spiritual renaissance is certainly not something I have only recently come to advocate in response to the present global crisis. In my first book, published in 1964, I wrote that 'There must now be many people who believe that a more constructive answer lies in the direction of what one may tentatively call a "radical spiritual renaissance", something deeper than a religious revival in the traditional sense, something involving the *whole* person.'

The passage of time has served to stress even more urgently the need for a more integrated perception of the world – a visionary form of politics more firmly rooted in morality and a spirituality more connected with social reality. One cannot now realistically envisage any such renaissance taking place apart from some kind of radical change in outlook regarding the perception of time.

Most of the actual writing of this book was done while I was living in a cottage in the foothills of the Black Mountains. On one side, down a steep bank, the River Monnow, which would turn into an angry russet torrent after heavy rain. Up above, on the other side, the mountains, with fields running up to them, then bracken and rocks.

As is usual in hill-farming communities, there is a spirit of cooperation among the farmers. Sometimes I gave a hand on my neighbour's farm during lambing, haymaking and shearing. Here one was constantly aware of nature and her changing moods – the sun glistening on the river in the morning, the wind and rain lashing down off the mountains, then the silence. An integral part of my life in this special place entailed simply watching, observing, feeling, allowing the stillness around me to seep into me and, hopefully, find its way onto the page.

At the more conscious level, this particular experiment with time began in the seventies, when I was living on the south-west coast of Ireland. Where more appropriate to ponder the mysteries of time? In any area where fishing and farming are the main activities, one soon becomes aware of the seasonal rhythm, the more cyclical aspect of time: there is a time to cut the turf, a time to fish mackerel, a time to make hay, a time to withdraw from the storms.

I spent many timeless moments up on the hills, watching the gannets spiralling upwards, then suddenly folding their wings and plummeting into the sea where they had spotted a shoal of mackerel. After a while they would clumsily re-emerge, slowly start flapping their wings, skimming over the waves and then spiralling upwards again. I read learned books on time, but the gannets taught me something different.

I

INNER-OUTER CONNECTIONS

We generally tend to overlook the political implications of our inner experiences, whether positive or negative. For practical purposes we divide events into two separate realms: interior, private, individual, personal and exterior, public, social, political. We use this working model so automatically that we forget that it results in a perception of the world that is refracted through dualistic lenses. We superimpose onto one world a split view of two worlds and as a result we might adopt a rigid either/or approach: if something is personal it cannot by definition be political.

This is both illogical in principle and invalid in practice. There is in reality no such clear dividing line separating the two worlds, which is not to deny individual identity or the need for privacy in the ordinary sense. Inner and outer processes are in fact continuously interacting and affecting each other, the outside world being shaped by what goes on in our inner spaces both consciously and unconsciously.

Whenever we focus unduly on one world to the exclusion of the other we obtain an unbalanced view of reality. For those who focus exclusively on spirituality and/or inner growth, 'politics' is a dirty word; while the political activist who ignores inner potential is likely to regard the whole idea of growth and/or spirituality as self-indulgent and élitist.

The ideal is a form of politics rooted in maturity and

higher values. These do not grow on trees. We have to work for them and most of the work is internal, involving the way we think and feel and perceive the external world.

The more extreme the dissociation and the more rigidly we believe in two radically separate worlds, the more powerless we feel as individuals in the face of all the global threats and ever-multiplying varieties of ecological destruction.

The more integrated our vision of the world, the more responsible we feel for the planet as a whole, the more involved we become and the more clearly we perceive the connection between inner and outer processes. The outside world is a reflection of what is happening in our inner worlds. As within so without and vice versa. There is also a timeless sense in which a given individual at a given time represents all persons at all times. The joys and sorrows of the human drama continue much as they ever have, regardless of how technologically sophisticated a given society might be.

As a direct result of events in our own inner spaces, we become more aware of human potential and take appropriate action in the outer spaces of society. Interconnectedness ceases to be merely a nice idea; it becomes part of our own direct experience of reality.

For example, whenever we have a peak experience we feel inwardly liberated. Such joyous moments are also often accompanied by a strong sense of unity with others, sometimes amounting to a certainty that separateness and disconnectedness are idiotic illusions. Peace ceases to be a remote ideal, a distant dream, and is experienced as present reality in the form of inner stillness and tranquillity. There may also be an almost overwhelming feeling of compassion, accompanied by total absence of any kind of fear.

Perceptual clarity of this kind is likely to lead to greatly enhanced social and global concern. The world out there is no longer perceived as something detached from oneself, one's own little world. The true spirit of politics cannot be rooted in disconnected abstract theories, however lofty and noble. It can only be based on directly experienced reality and this involves the most precious of all freedoms – inner liberation.

At the negative end of the spectrum, a person suffering from depression, for example, feels weighed down by an overwhelming sense of unworthiness and weakness. This is often accompanied by a feeling of acute isolation and separation from others, those physically close to one and the world in general. Underlying the angst there may be a potential volcano of unacknowledged and repressed anger, in the form of unresolved inner conflicts. The more this rage festers and builds up in the unconscious, the more potentially destructive it becomes. The repressed anger might suddenly and unexpectedly erupt in an irrational outburst of unrestrained fury, or it might be turned inwards and take the form of a suicide attempt.

Nation-states that might normally convey an impression of reason and moderation can sometimes become gripped by a terrible collective frenzy, as in the first world war when the young men of whole nations were despatched to slaughter and be slaughtered. Collective madness is always easier to identify at a different time in history, or in any nation but one's own. But it is also present in a more disguised form in one's own nation, now, when so-called 'defence' policies involve the willingness both to perpetrate mass murder against whole populations as well as to commit mass suicide. Similar if not identical psychological terminology can be used with regard to both the individual and the nation-state.

Whenever we feel depressed we also feel disempowered, politically disenfranchised, and lose faith in our ability to take any kind of action for change to the better. We may become passive and apathetic, absorbing all the bad news of which there is never any shortage and taking a cynical view of 'human nature'. The state of the world certainly is depressing and it is easy to feel overwhelmed by massive audiovisual exposure to bad news. Sometimes we need all the inner resources at our disposal to stay centred, to retain a sense of balance and keep things in proportion.

The western psyche has been traumatized as one mind. As members of society we are all part of the crises of our society. We are all born into a wounded culture. Two world wars, Auschwitz and Hiroshima have left wounds so deep that many seek to deny that such wounds even exist. No healing can take place under a cover-up of pretence and the first step towards healing is to recognize the existence of wounds. This applies to whole societies in much the same way as to individuals.

Just as in the life of an individual it might require a major crisis of some kind to shift a person's worldview, prejudices and strongly held beliefs, so the whole outlook of a given society can change in a more benign direction when the positive potential of a crisis is seen more clearly for what it actually is: a time of opportunity.

Time and history

One can distinguish two main schools of thought regarding the perception of time and history. Those in power have an obvious vested interest in maintaining a business-as-usual approach, which is fundamental to the smooth running of a consumerist economy, which is in turn conducive to the kind of inner repression of the human spirit necessary to maintain the status quo. Growth and healing involve change and change of the status quo is something all powerbrokers would rather do without.

Throughout the Christian centuries, when the Church wielded power, the ecclesiastical establishment had an obvious vested interest in drastically restricting the higher vision. Clearly the whole hierarchical, pyramid-shaped structure would have been completely undermined by popular mysticism, by significant numbers of people realizing their higher potential. For many centuries it was politically expedient to marginalize the higher vision, restricting it to a very small élite of officially approved saints and contemplatives. This gave the general impression that the experience concerned (inner liberation) was exceedingly rare and reserved only for those in a near-perfect state of grace, in other words hardly anybody. For ecclesiastical powerbrokers the business-as-usual school entailed an exceedingly narrow and restricted view of human potential.

The traditional teaching of the Church, for so long enforced under pain of death, has inevitably left its mark. The shape of the pyramid has been branded into the western psyche and we live in a society that still assumes that this must for ever be the shape of political reality.

Just as the whole pyramid power structure of the Church would have been undermined by widespread popular mysticism, so the structure of the modern state is equally threatened when people begin to realize their true inner potential. As a result of many centuries of cultural conditioning and of allowing repressive assumptions to be passed on unchallenged from generation to generation, we continue to deny our own higher potential. Because this is not acknowledged as a natural part of our inner reality, we tend to project it in a distorted, refracted form on to external leader figures. Not very surprisingly we then become somewhat disillusioned with the whole political process.

The other main perception is based on the view that Hiroshima represents the most crucial watershed in western history, the most radical break in our time. It also serves as a warning to the species in general and our culture in particular, showing us all the possibility of evil on a scale that would completely dwarf Auschwitz. There is ample firepower to produce the equivalent of over a million Hiroshimas. Over a million Hiroshimas. . . One cannot comprehend the enormity of such evil. Yet we live with this evil *now,* continuously, day and night, at every moment, since it is a well established and basic moral principle that the willingness or intention to commit an evil act is in itself evil.

Most people regard themselves as apolitical. Yet in taking no action to change the status quo they are thereby prolonging its existence, which is a highly political thing to be doing. It is a fallacy to suppose that if one is not being overtly political, one is thereby somehow excluded from the political process as a whole. The deprivation of power is just as political as the exercise of power. We are by nature socio-political animals and our lives are constantly and continuously bound up with the political process, power, who wields it and how, who doesn't and why not.

The way we perceive politics is fundamental to the kind of society we live in, the quality of life or its absence. When issues of life and death, human survival, good planet management, morality, compassion, vision and inspiration are all marginalized away from the political mainstream, the meagre remnants are something other than true politics. If the political process ceases to be primarily and fundamentally concerned with life itself, in its deepest and richest sense, then the insipid left-overs are merely pseudo-political shadows of the real thing.

Although we all live in a particular country with its own nationalistic definition of patriotism, we are also world citizens and fellow inhabitants of this relatively small and highly vulnerable planet. Yet we have barely begun to think in terms of re-defining patriotism in more globally appropriate ways. As world citizens the area over which most of the people are least represented most of the time is morality – the morality of planet management and human survival.

The most obvious global morality test for any political party is its policy on nuclear weapons. When a given 'defence' policy involves the willingness to participate in the greatest possible crime against humanity – its extinction – it represents the politics of repression. The repression in this instance is more subtle, more covert and hidden than the more obvious kinds of repression western leaders were so good at selectively identifying in the eastern bloc. It entails repression of the human spirit, higher values – moral and metaphysical repression.

Western glasnost

Whereas the eastern version of *glasnost* (openness) applies to the more obvious failings of the Soviet political process, its western equivalent has a more subtle meaning: allowing our higher faculties to develop, being more open about our latent visionary potential, no longer hiding our lights under bushels, stating our higher needs more forthrightly and vigorously and demanding political representation of those needs.

The moment we start to apply *glasnost* in this deeper sense to ourselves, we see that we have allowed the moralist in us to remain too silent for too long in the face of the greatest evils. Sanctimonious and holier-than-thou finger-pointing on the part of western leaders served to distract public attention from the continuous inner repression of the human spirit in western consumerist society.

The great majority of MPs in this country still support NATO, which operates a policy of first use of nuclear weapons. If applied this would result in a major nuclear exchange between the superpowers, with Europe in the middle. This would – or at least could – result in the ultimate crime of omnicide, the death of all.

There is currently a thaw in east-west relations. But it would probably only require an incident or two to bring all the cold warriors out of the woodwork again, and we might be back in the bad old days of 'evil empire' rhetoric. Despite the current improvement in international relations, as far as NATO war planners and strategists are concerned the perceived threat from the east is as great as ever. It has to be seen this way, otherwise continued arms escalation by stealth – the so-called 'modernization' and 'compensatory' programmes – would not seem to be justified. There still has to be a baddy, the red demon, over there in the east. After all, the NATO exercises have to have an enemy, and all the low-flying air sorties have to be seen to be 'defending' us against somebody. Besides, there is colossal vested interest in the perpetuation of the arms industry as a whole. For many powerful people the thought of the multitude of scientists and technicians involved in this gargantuan death industry suddenly being out of a job is something more dreadful to contemplate than the prospect of universal destruction.

Omnicide

The term 'omnicide' was coined some time ago by the American philosopher, John Somerville, in an attempt to bring greater linguistic honesty to bear on discourse concerning the nuclear issue.[1] The nuclear debate is usually conducted within the parameters of a mentality belonging to the old order, when wars could still be fought between nations without threatening the whole planet and human survival itself. This no longer applies and it is incorrect and dishonest to continue to talk in terms of nuclear 'war', when in reality what is being referred to is something other than war. When we substitute the word 'omnicide' for 'war' we get a more accurate picture of the real situation, as opposed to the war-game fantasy scenarios conjured up by strategists in bunkers playing around with video screens. Clearly we cannot talk in terms of 'winning' nuclear omnicide, or fighting a 'just' nuclear omnicide. To continue to refer to universal death as war has the effect of prolonging cold war psychology, thereby carrying over into the post-Hiroshima age attitudes and ways of thinking belonging to the old order.

When political leaders state their willingness to 'press the button' they are expressing an intention to perpetrate omnicide. As already stated, it is a well established moral principle that the clear intention to commit an evil act is in itself evil.

All talk of a political party trying to gain the 'moral high ground' is meaningless if the party in question advocates a 'defence' policy based on absolute evil.

State violence tends to condone individual violence, whether the officially sanctioned violence concerns a single death, as with capital punishment, or species death, as with omnicide. If the tribal elders of a given society are prepared to commit acts of absolute evil, this affects the whole tone of life for those in that society. It may not be expressed explicitly, but at the back of people's minds lurks the notion that if the supposed guardians of the state are living, day in day out, with this absolutely evil intention, then acts of relative violence at an individual level seem both permissible and inevitable.

The rise in violent crime, terrorism, football hooliganism and the general expectation of ever-increasing levels of violence all take place in the shadow of the pyramid of absolute violence. Those at the top of the pyramid who advocate policies involving the use of absolute violence are thus hardly in a strong moral position to condemn acts of relative violence. All the latter take place within the overall perspective of the political willingness to bring about universal destruction.

The chauvinist mentality of the football thugs reflects the national chauvinism of those who still believe in the 'British bomb'. Dave Hill points out that the bitter pill which government, football authorities and media alike do not wish to swallow is that the hooligan code of values 'is uncomfortably like a mutated reflection of their own'. The thug thinks of himself as a super-patriot and cannot understand why flag-waving 'patriotism' is considered acceptable during the Falklands War, but unacceptable when expressed violently on the streets of a German town.[2]

This cultural chauvinism dovetailed neatly into the post-war psychology of the cold war. The 'Reds' were identified with the whole of the Soviet Union in an undifferentiated way. Only such indiscriminate chauvinism could have allowed war establishments on both sides to get away with the monstrously unnecessary escalation of the arms race.

No matter what is going on at any given time at summit meetings between superpower leaders, the risk of omnicide remains as long as the old nation-state war mentality continues to be carried over into the post-Hiroshima world in which we now live. If we are really serious about wanting to get rid of the risk of omnicide, we have to explore the mentality underlying all wars – the sort of psychological attitude that is conducive to the conduct of war, ways of thinking that convey the impression that warmaking is a permanent and ineradicable feature of the human condition.

Final solutions

We belong to a century that would appear to have specialized in the refinement and perfection of final solutions. The first world war was seen by many as the war to end wars, the final solution of war itself. Far from ending war, the unjust post-war settlements led inexorably to the second world war, which in turn led equally inexorably to the cold war, the all-but-declared third world war. Not long after the allies had discovered the truth about Hitler's attempted genocidal final solution, the dropping of the atomic bomb on Hiroshima ushered in the age of omnicide, the attempted final solution of the tiresome old world and all its hitherto insoluble problems.

It is not straightforward rapaciousness and greed that are destroying the planet. These are only the more obvious outward and visible expressions of a world-hating manichaean demon lurking in the shadows of the western collective psyche. The power-wielders and decision-makers act out like blind automata the repressed demonic processes in our psyches. If we could recognize and acknowledge our own western demons, no matter how strange they might be, they would then no longer possess us, driving us on ever closer to the abyss and making us perform acts totally contrary to our own better natures. There is virtually universal agreement that the present situation is both mad and bad, but very little insight into its underlying causes.

The portals of insight are firmly closed if we conclude, with dogmatic finality, that speculation is merely an élitist luxury reserved for affluent city-dwellers with plenty of good food and wine in their stomachs. Today's global problems are so immense that we now have to 'think big', rekindle our visionary faculties and vastly expand our mental horizons if we are to come anywhere near doing justice to the scale of the problems facing us all.

Without a reasonable degree of insight we are merely reacting to the last link in the causal chain, by which time the whole destructive process is well under way. In order to stop the varieties of destruction at their sources, we have to be prepared to explore deep levels of the western psyche, to explore our own minds. When we connect our own inner experience with outside events in the world, we find ourselves engaged in an open-ended exploration which by its very nature can have no final solution.

There would appear to be an underlying feature in our western culture conducive to the repression of higher values on a scale vast enough to permit the idea of final solutions to be part and parcel of the conventional worldview. A fundamental prerequisite of the final solution mentality is a repressive view of time. This is precisely what we find in our western culture – a view of time that stands out from other cultural perceptions for its unbalanced linear chronological reductionism. The conventional notion of time involves stressing the horizontal aspect to the near-total exclusion of the vertical – those temporal perspectives that connect everyday existence to higher values, that endow our ordinary activities with deeper meaning.

Time is every society's hidden agenda. Religious symbolism is essentially a statement about the perceived nature of time, indicating how the people of a given society react to the process with which their lives are intimately bound up from the moment of birth until the moment of death. Thus when we unravel what a society says or fails to say about time, we thereby gain some insight into the inner state of the society concerned. What it fails to say can be more significant than explicit time language.

The willingness to perpetrate the most criminally insane acts seems in our case to be rooted in the very measure of our concept of normality, accurate chronological measurement being essential to the highly scheduled existence of a modern urban-industrial society. We assume that without our ultra-narrow concept of time, everything would grind to a halt. But our government's economic and 'defence' policies, which are so efficient and highly scheduled, are themselves ensuring that everything will sooner rather than later grind to a halt anyway.

Needless to say it is not a question of attempting to 'abolish time', cast aside our watches and 'do a Rousseau'. Instead it involves a recovery of temporal balance, the restoration of the vertical aspects.

There is of course no final solution to the 'time problem'. Time will always remain an unfathomable mystery; the more we explore it, the more aware we become of its mysterious nature. It is when the whole of time is reduced to and identified with only one aspect of it that the trouble starts. Only a society that suffers from the delusion that it can finally solve anything so mysterious and insoluble as time is capable of thinking in terms of perpetrating final solutions on the mystery of life itself. As St Augustine humbly admitted, there is an intuitive sense in which we know what we know about time, but as soon as we try to express this verbally we are lost for words.

Scientists know more than the rest of us about quantum theory, but this is only one facet of time and we are certainly not disqualified from the experiment with time simply because we may not be experts in this particular field. In reality, we are all experts on the experiential aspect of time – the time of everyday life. This is our own direct, real, down-to-earth experience and as such it is closer to nature and reality than many of the more abstract and arcane time theories and is in this sense empirical and scientific.

But once any society believes that an élitist little group is privy to some kind of secret knowledge, then the members of the society in question abrogate some of their own inner moral authority and hand it over to the shamans of the day. This disempowerment of the individual involves the repression of the vertical aspect of time. This greater time was traditionally held to belong to the 'next world' and was consequently projected away from this timeworld. Today such a world is not held to exist at all, anywhere. Psychologically the effect is the same: the repression or denial of the higher vision.

The repression takes place at a deep level and is essentially metaphysical. It concerns time, timelessness, existence, non-existence, God, eternity, meaning, meaninglessness, life and death. When we stop exploring these processes we repress the metaphysician in ourselves and push away, relegate to the outer fringes, processes that in reality and in any healthy society belong right in the very centre of social and political life.

The notion that metaphysical speculation is an élitist luxury misses the whole point, quite apart from being untrue anyway. Nomadic desert cultures, for example, have integrated metaphysics with their everyday lives. It is precisely because they have such a balanced view of time, incorporating the vertical aspect (what the aborigines call the Dream Time) into their daily activities, that they can carry on at all, because their way of life has deeper meaning for them. When they give this up, lead a more settled and comfortable existence and become initiated into the ways of the west, they tend to lose sight of this sacred inner core of meaning (since they are plunged into a culture that exalts the horizontal aspect of time to the exclusion of the vertical). As a result they often give up, lose their previous zest for life and spiral downwards into despair and alcoholism.

In suffering from the delusion that our advanced society has found the final solution to the 'time problem' merely by achieving near-perfect chronological measurement, we bring our own experiments with time to an end, thereby depriving our lives of deeper meaning and turning ourselves into passive spectators rather than active participants in the shaping of our own society. We then wonder why modern life in general and modern political life in particular are so often so arid, so insipid, so lacking in vision and inspiration. We can hardly expect our political representatives to be visionaries if we suppress and deny the visionary in ourselves.

In *The Nature of Time,* G. J. Whitrow observes that the notion that time is a kind of linear progression measured by the clock and calendar so dominates our lives that it gives the impression of being an inescapable necessity of thought. But this is far from true, since most civilizations prior to our own of the last two or three hundred years have tended to regard time as essentially cyclic in nature: 'In the light of history, our conception of time is as exceptional as our rejection of magic'.[3] But to live a highly scheduled, completely clockwork sort of existence is itself a superstition, a form of magic disguised by the glossy front of modern technology. In our cultural arrogance we like to think that only 'primitive' cultures go in for superstition.

Throughout the medieval period, cyclical and linear views of time were in conflict. The scientists and scholars tended to favour the cyclical approach, whereas the linear view was backed by the mercantile class and was ideally suited to the rise of a money economy. The merchants of course won the argument and our notion of time has ever since retained its more mercantile attributes, pecuniary and temporal expressions being interchangeable.

Macho time

It was only during the course of the seventeenth century that the idea of linear progress began to play such a dominant role in western thinking. In 1602 Bacon published a work entitled *The Masculine Birth of Time* – a title which accurately reflected what was then taking place. The whole notion of progress became increasingly identified with a macho-aggressive, conquering outlook.

The first thing one observes on investigating the cosmologies and creation myths of other cultures is how abnormal our western view of time is in relation to other temporal norms. The extreme abnormality of our present historical situation is rooted in the abnormality of our view of time. A society that does not place the same great emphasis as ours on the concept of absolute beginnings and final solutions would have great difficulty in finding itself where we are now, faced with the prospect of global destruction. A society that had succeeded in retaining the balance between the vertical and horizontal, retaining images and metaphors connecting the greater time (macro time) with everyday time (micro time), would not be capable of thinking apocalyptically and as a result arranging its military strategy accordingly.

Our notion of time has mainly been shaped by the judaeo-christian tradition and its cosmology of creation *ex nihilo* and final annihilation – the Genesis-Apocalypse worldview, with the beginning connected to the end by a one-way timeline, which in turn shapes our western idea of causality, cause and effect, one thing after another. Quite instinctively we use apocalyptic language in everyday speech, expressions such as the 'end of the world', the 'end of time', or just 'the end'. We take such expressions so completely for granted that we tend to overlook the fact that the overwhelming majority of other societies do not think like this, do not see the world in terms of beginnings and ends with a one-way causal timeline running from start to finish.

From the eighteenth century onwards, the notions of never-ending industrial productivity and economic growth came to be seen as permanent features of western economies, regardless of whether or not products were good for those who bought them, benefited or harmed the planet, promoted peace or war.

The symbolic figures on the old clocks, which can still be seen in cathedrals and churches, in due course gave way to our more familiar purely functional timepieces. The change-over – from a representation of time that relates in some way to daily activities, to a portrayal of time unconnected to actual experience – inevitably involved the repression of vital connecting processes. Lewis Mumford went to the heart of the whole question of dissociation in observing that 'The clock dissociated time from human events and helped create the belief in an independent world of mathematically measurable sequences'.[4]

Once people start believing in separate, disconnected and independent worlds, the vital link between the micro time of everyday life (horizontal time) and the greater, macro time is severed. Once this has happened it is of course much easier to contemplate the destruction of the world out there, which is perceived as a completely separate entity unconnected with one's own inner timeworld. In order to carry out a really efficient demolition job on nature, it is first necessary to distance oneself from her. The natural world has to be perceived as detached from one's own world, otherwise commonsense self-interest would preclude any kind of all-embracing death wish, which would be seen for what it is: omnicidal and therefore also suicidal.

A culture with a more integrated worldview would no doubt continue to have the occasional defensive war, but it could not contemplate the final destruction of a world perceived as timeless and in some sense sacred and therefore eternal. Such destruction would not only be a contradiction in terms; it would represent the ultimate act of sacrilege.

It would be inconceivable. Via its war policies, which are predominantly offensive rather than genuinely defensive, a culture that subscribes to the notion of final solutions is seeking to impose its own apocalyptic cosmology on the whole world – on all other existing societies and potential future cultural developments, for all time. This represents the same *conquistador* mentality that led to the ruthless colonization of Latin America.

The survival of the planet is still not perceived by the majority as the most urgent issue, taking precedence over all others. Concern over the fate of the planet is displaced and expressed in other ways: people tend to worry more about their own immediate financial and consumerist concerns. Temporal dissociation (the creation of separate and independent timeworlds) induces psychological displacement on a scale massive enough to maintain the nuclear status quo. Even the biggest anti-nuclear demonstration only represents a small fraction of the actual anxiety in the general psyche. To put the same thing another way: if the majority actually faced the truth, confronted their own fear over the future and took appropriate political action, no government in the world could resist popular pressure on such a large scale.

Displacement

The consumerist ethos is of course ideally designed to induce displacement, diverting energy away from the most vital primary issue of survival. Underlying this psychological displacement process is temporal dissociation and its independent timeworlds, which in turn involve metaphysical repression – the denial of higher values and/or their projection away from this world onto another. It is in the interests of any modern government to promote displacement at every possible opportunity. Truth is the worst enemy of the nuclear state, which must always maintain secrecy, oppose freedom of information and define national security in terms of maintaining the status quo.

The entertainment industry and in particular television play major roles in the displacement process. The very act of viewing, regardless of what appears on the screen, is consumerist-passive rather than creator-active. The body language expresses a frame of mind: in shutting the curtains and settling down to an evening in front of the telly, one is symbolically telling the rest of the world out there and all its problems to go to hell. Also the whole concept of producing programmes is by its very nature a time-filling exercise. All that empty space must be filled. The underlying ideology is anything but neutral: it presupposes that time is something that has to be filled in and killed.

Since displacement is an essential part of a worldview that gives the impression that war is a permanent feature of the human landscape, the way we perceive time and try and manipulate it according to our cultural ideologies is far from neutral. Anything that promotes displacement is politically biased in favour of the conduct of war.

The old war time norm has a built-in bias masquerading outwardly as neutrality, balance, objectivity, normality. It is therefore inevitable that attempts to find a more genuinely centred position seem 'politically biased', if not 'subversive', to those who have moved the goal-posts well to the right of centre. Peace studies and any genuinely objective exploration of war and conflict are bound to seem 'politically biased' to those who regard war as the norm.

The old battle history approach to the story of humankind, which reigned supreme in the classroom for generations, was a highly selective account heavily biased in a pessimistic direction. A negative judgement on the species, based on the 'beast in man' myth, had been passed beforehand, so the evidence had to be selected accordingly to support this prejudiced view.

The limitless expanses of timespace between outward and

visible events seemed dull and lacking in action compared to the 'history of action man' – the endless succession of wars and battles. The impression was conveyed that the timespace between battles must by nature be dull, since the battles were exciting and conveyed a picture of action. War is the most easily observed historical expression of action; these reactionary history lessons inevitably conveyed the impression that war action is somehow commendable, while the apparent inaction of peace is boring.

The interior life, with its far more subtle, often highly paradoxical, psychological and metaphysical processes, is of course just as valid and real a part of the human story as the more easily observed, more quantifiable exterior manifestations of human behaviour. The description of a given event, such as a battle, reveals only a very small part of the tip of the iceberg of the totality of human processes, the overwhelming majority of which are hidden, invisible and usually enshrouded in impenetrable mystery. A battle is a mere fragment of an event that is itself the last expression of a preceding infinite series of highly complex processes. A battle, whether fought with bows and arrows or modern weapons, represents the most visible, most perceptually accessible, least subtle, least paradoxical stage in a vastly complex, highly subtle and extremely paradoxical preceding internal process.

Our western history has hitherto been seen in a highly visibilist way: the emphasis has been on the most obvious facts to the detriment of less visible processes, which to the reductionist are not even facts because of their invisibility. The mechanistic-reductionist worldview is expressed most obviously in the high technology computerized world of contemporary military strategy. The more modern gadgetry is inserted between the killer and the killed, the less the killer worries about killing. The modern commander can sit back and have a cup of coffee as he selects the appropriate programme for destroying cities. He looks at his screen and just sees cyphers, digits, symbols – which actually represent human beings.

Modern war technology carries spatio-temporal dissociation to its ultimate limits. To the modern strategist, there are no people out there – only a bunch of impersonal statistics marked 'enemy'. Being the enemy, they must be destroyed as efficiently as possible. This involves turning the reality of one timeworld into several separate fantasy timeworlds. It is obviously a lot easier to blow to smithereens a timeworld seen as a mere fantasy than to perceive oneself more connected to one's actions and thereby to realize that by pressing the button, one is actually blowing *one's own* world to bits.

The greatest illusion of all, of course, is to believe that a machine can give human advice based on human value judgements. As Michael Shallis reminds us in *The Silicon Idol,* 'advice' from a machine will always be untrustworthy because it can never include the very factors that go to make up human experience. Over-dependence on machine advice leads not entirely surprisingly to inhuman, mechanistic, reductionist action. The humans responsible then sometimes try and blame the machine.

Shallis describes how, during the Vietnam War, computers made 'judgements' as to which villages should be bombed. Decisions taken as a result of such 'judgements' meant that people were killed, maimed and rendered homeless and no person was responsible – a machine was. The computers were programmed to 'lie' to the policy decision-makers about what targets had been bombed. For quite a long time the secret bombing of Cambodia went undetected, because details of each bombing mission were falsified by the computer and converted into so-called 'legitimate' (i.e. Vietnamese) targets: 'Thus the computer rearranges reality and "creates" history.'[5]

The truth is of course that reality cannot be artificially rearranged; nor can history be created by machines. The

actual reality of our story consists mainly of limitless tracts
of timespace with no convenient outwardly visible markers
of any kind whatever. The true human story does not consist
of win-or-lose certainties like battles – clearcut, either/or,
non-paradoxical situations. The only historical certainty is
uncertainty. But the western branch of the species suffers
from an aversion against uncertainty, paradox, mystery,
timelessness, emptiness, nothingness. The old patriarchal
pyramid structure, where everybody thought they knew
exactly where they stood – God in his heaven, rich man in
his castle, the poor at the gate – such a rigid structure provided the reassuring role of appearing to fill the empty void.

The only way of being certain that awkward paradoxes can
be finally eliminated is to eliminate finally all those capable of
perceiving such untidy, illogical and mysterious phenomena.
The death of all (omnicide) represents the final solution of
the insoluble. There would appear to lurk in the western
psyche a malign demon so certain of its hatred of uncertainty
that it wants to be absolutely certain of never having to face
another paradox ever again.

But the event that took place on 6 August 1945 represents
a whole cluster of paradoxes – just about everything the
western mind has been taught to reject. So rather than face
this supreme mystery of one form of time ending and another
beginning, we pretend that business carries on as usual as
though nothing particularly untoward has happened. We
only see what we want to see and in this respect are like
those antipodean islanders who did not even 'see' Captain
Cook's vessels when they first appeared. Such phenomena
were so completely outside their conventional ways of
seeing, their habitual mind sets, that they did not even bother
to look up.

The repression of timeless values

In order to be able to bring about a situation of absolute evil and total destruction, something timeless and universal has to be denied or repressed on a proportionately vast scale. The massive scale of the threatened physical destruction indicates the extent of the metaphysical repression that underlies it. The physical overkill capacity reflects the scale of the overkill of timeless values.

The need for higher values is as natural and normal a part of being human as any other need. The more the higher needs are denied, repressed or projected away from us and our timeworld, the less we value ourselves, each other, our time, our space, our world. The motivation to preserve the species and its habitat is obviously greatly weakened if we ascribe no kind of higher value to either. Omnicidal policies are rooted in metaphysical repression. To eliminate the threat of omnicide we have to eliminate the mentality underlying it.

Fossilized structures from bygone days ensure that higher values are kept well away from the sociopolitical mainstream of daily life. The world beyond time is thus effectively insulated from the real world, timeless values usually being wrapped up in cocoons marked 'religion' and 'art'. When we start to unwrap these cocoons we see that the underlying processes are in fact universal and should therefore be accessible to everybody, regardless of formal church allegiance, or whether or not one sees oneself as artistic.

Creator and consumer

'Creativity' is often defined in an élitist and disconnected way. 'Art' tends to be seen as something highbrow and musty that goes on in museums and art galleries, rather than a living process integrated with life. The creative artist is usually seen as a special kind of person, whereas every person is in reality a special kind of artist, of one sort or another.

If we allowed expression to the creator in us, we would observe a different flow of energy that could be socially transformative. Consumer energy is dissipated in the never-ending quest for new products and is essentially selfish. Creative energy focuses on processes beyond the ego and is potentially altruistic, outward-going rather than grasping. The consumer in us is always at the receiving end of whatever is being consumed – food or products – and is essentially passive. The creator is an active initiator of new processes and original ideas. The consumer in us takes, while the creator gives.

Those with the strongest vested interest in a consumerist economy obviously stand to gain most in always ensuring that the consumer receives priority, which in turn entails the repression of higher values. The moment universal values ceased to be marginalized away from the social, economic and political mainstream, people would soon start noticing that they could be more content leading a simpler lifestyle with only the basic essentials, rather than a vast array of products, most of which are totally unnecessary and many of which are positively harmful. The political and economic repercussions of such awareness would be considerable: people would very soon cease to believe in the myth of never-ending economic growth.

In the late seventies, when decision-makers and powerful people from American presidents downwards began talking in terms of Small is Beautiful, the economic powerbrokers began to get a little anxious. There was real fear in some of the multinational boardrooms that Fritz Schumacher's lecture tours in America might actually result in radical political action of some kind. Barbara Wood describes in her biography how Schumacher was suddenly provided with a police escort and threats that had been made on his life began to be taken seriously by the authorities.

> There were suggestions that his opponents came from the
> most powerful industrial and business interests in the United
> States, who recognized the danger to their existence if Fritz's
> message really caught on and became policy and practice.
> They did not like to be told that the idolatry of giantism was
> responsible for 'a system of production that ravishes nature
> and a type of society that mutilates man'.[6]

Any modern government would of course far prefer
people to devote most of their energy to consumerism than
planetary survival. Once people start to be concerned about
the fate of the earth, they begin to connect things. Once this
process starts, people are well on the way to being politicized
and re-empowered. They then observe how repressed they
had been before and wonder why they had not done something about this repression much sooner.

When one investigates possible reasons inhibiting people
from changing their worldviews and self-images from consu-
mer-dominant to creator-dominant, one finds that fear of
social disapproval is one of the most powerful blockages.
The more conventional and conformist the social environment, the more people will tend to regard creative artists as
non-conformists, eccentrics, weird, anti-social perhaps. It is
therefore hardly surprising to learn that when researchers
explore the more visionary and transcendental aspects of
human experience, they encounter strong cultural taboos.
There is widespread reluctance even to admit experiences
related to heightened states of awareness, moments of illumination and profound liberation. Nobody wants to be considered a crank, least of all a 'mystic' – a term which is
usually used in a derogatory way, especially in reductionist
circles. We lack a positive vocabulary for this aspect of our
lives, so we tend to deny such things altogether.

The most dangerous and sinister aspect of this repression
is that otherwise normal, healthy processes re-emerge in
bizarre and destructive forms. We do not lack evidence that
this happens frequently and have only to think of the multi-

tude of millennarian and messianic cults in America, the television evangelists and their high-pressure fund raising, the Jim Joneses of this world. David Hay, a leading researcher in this field, stresses that 'Human realities which are resolutely ignored tend to return in bizarre or fanatical forms'.

The destructive effects of the repression and denial of human realities extend very much further than bizarre and fanatical forms of religion. What must rank as the most deeply repressive of all cultures has so far this century produced two world wars, the Nazi holocaust, Hiroshima and the constant threat of omnicide. The deeper the repression, the more destructive the effects.

Myths and misperceptions are of course far more powerful determinants of behaviour than actual experience. The myth that science involves rigid conformity to reductionist norms is more widespread than the true spirit of science, which involves fearless and open-minded inquiry, no matter where this might lead. Hay observes that the norm to which people seem to feel they must conform is a reductionist one:

> Our everyday world of meanings is modelled on ways of thinking which give success in the scientific and technological manipulation of matter and energy. We volunteer to confine ourselves to those parts of reality which are clear, distinct, measurable and therefore examinable by the methods of empirical science . . . The pressure to conform is now not simply a matter of fitting one's deeper experience into a pre-determined religious mould, but to deny utterly its validity or its existence.[7]

The good name of science is also sometimes misappropriated in order to give the appearance of justifying ultra-aggressive strategic policies. This particularly applies to the notion of the 'biological roots of aggression'. This concept is sometimes dressed up in seemingly plausible scientific attire, but in reality it is a very old myth long pre-dating the advent of modern scientific methodology. It is quite simply the re-appearance of the doctrine of original sin in more secular garb, the 'beast in man' myth in modern dress.

The 'beast in man' myth

In 1986 a gathering of behavioural scientists at Seville felt it necessary to make a statement on violence. This was an attempt to set the record straight and counteract the tendency to try and justify war and oppression in the name of science. The statement reminds us that it is scientifically incorrect to say that we have inherited a tendency to make war from our animal ancestors, that it is equally incorrect to claim that war or any other violent behaviour is genetically programmed into our human nature, or to claim that humans have some kind of a 'violent brain'. The Seville Statement concluded that 'There is nothing in our neurophysiology that compels us to react violently . . . Biology does not condemn humanity to war'.[8]

The popular perception is very different. Most people still suffer from the delusion that war is somehow an inescapable part of 'human nature' and that there is therefore no realistic alternative to a 'tough' defence policy of deterrence. In advocating this, the proponents seem to overlook the fact that this whole posture is not remotely defensive, but highly offensive and threatening, thereby forcing the perceived enemy to react accordingly.

Theories of human evolution are basically creation myths, stories about the first appearance of humans on earth. Mary Midgley stresses this mythical aspect of science in the opening lines of *Evolution as a Religion:*

> The theory of evolution is not just an inert piece of theoretical science. It is, and cannot help being, also a powerful folk-tale about human origins. Any such narrative must have symbolic force . . . Suggestions about how we were made and where we came from are bound to engage our

imagination, to shape our views of what we now are, and so to affect our lives.[9]

Theories on human origins often turn out on closer inspection to tell us more about the social attitudes prevailing at the time than about our earlier ancestors. It is only relatively recently that researchers have become aware of the ideological content of many scientific theories. The doctrine of original sin was of course very much part of the whole cultural landscape in Darwin's day and was inevitably absorbed by most of the early evolutionists to be re-stated in a more naturalistic way.

Theories on human aggression became a mirror which reflected only those aspects of behaviour which its authors wanted to tell. A self-selecting image of 'human nature' was built up in the popular mind. It was a deeply pessimistic image. How we see ourselves and our potential, or lack of it, has a direct bearing on what we achieve, or fail to. As long ago as 1740 the dissenting divine John Taylor put it succinctly when he asked: 'What can be more destructive of virtue than to have a notion that you must, in some degree or other, be necessarily vicious?'[10]

Once the myth of the fall became formalized as the doctrine of original sin it became inevitable that time would come to be perceived within the cultural context of a fallen world. If members of a given society see themselves as inherently corrupt, weak and sinful, they are inclined to see the world and its time (their timeworld) through pessimistic lenses. The time of this world thus came to be seen as nasty, brutish and short, while the time of the next was seen as nice, angelic and long.

Sacred eternal time was kept locked away in a separate place and only church officials held the sacramental key. A more effective system of metaphysical bondage would be hard to imagine, with the spiritual power concentrated in Rome. Patriarchal and hierarchical images were projected onto the next world and the resulting picture was highly anthropomorphic: God the Father was King and Lord of the eternal Kingdom, His Son sitting next to Him, with serried ranks of celestial beings in descending order of seniority – archangels, angels, saints and lesser beatified souls. Sacred time was turned into a place which was located very far away from this fallen world and its sin-ridden inhabitants.

The idea that there are two radically separate timeworlds – the 'profane' time of this world and the sacred time of the next – is the most deeply rooted of our western archetypes. All the most destructive of our misperceptions have their roots in this the greatest misperception of all. The splitting of time underlies our other more familiar dualistic splits, profoundly affecting our whole outlook, how we perceive the world and its time, how we see the idea of the 'end of the world' and, above all, how we think we think – how we perceive the thought process itself. Until this is at least to some degree clarified, we cannot expect to have a clear view of anything else.

II

THE REINTEGRATION OF VALUES

In *The Yogi and the Commissar*, Arthur Koestler used two figures at extreme opposite ends of the spectrum to stress the need for some kind of rapprochement between the best of the two worlds, spiritual and temporal, religious and political. As a former active communist, Koestler had experienced the Stalinist commissar mentality at first hand. He had seen too many who had started their political careers imbued with idealism and a strong sense of social responsibility, who had formed bonds of fraternal solidarity while plotting the revolution in dank cellars, but who, once the revolution in question had succeeded, turned on their former comrades, betrayed them and their own ideals, grew paranoid and scorned any form of morality.

Koestler's yogi is an idealist in the philosophical sense: if enemy tanks are rolling into town, he just sits there impassively in a state of contemplative inertia. There is no point in taking any action, since the tanks are mere illusions anyway. This extreme quietist guru figure symbolizes denial of the reality of matter, time and history.

The affairs of this world are essentially a bad dream; only the spiritual world is real. The only kind of change possible for the yogi is individual change from within and he is totally committed to the belief that ends, no matter how noble, never justify the use of violent and/or immoral means.

The commissar, on the other hand, believes only in matter and regards the iron laws of historical determinism as forming the basis of the revolution. He is totally committed to external, structural, social and political change and believes that the attainment of his particular version of Utopia justifies the use of any means under the sun, no matter how violent and/or immoral.

Saint and revolutionary

The main point Koestler is trying to make is that politics needs to recover its own deeper roots and moral connections in order to ensure that the exercise of power always remains firmly anchored in the soil of wisdom and compassion. Neither the spiritual aspect of life in isolation nor the political severed from morality can achieve this desirable state of affairs, only some kind of connection between the best of both worlds: 'Neither the saint nor the revolutionary can save us; only the synthesis of the two'.[1]

Whether or not the saint–revolutionary synthesis is desirable, let alone possible, depends on how you define the processes represented by these two words. There is no shortage of historical and contemporary examples of the combination of the worst of both worlds – fanatical religious zealots regarded by their followers as saints, who wield power with the ruthlessness of the old–style commissar.

At each extreme of the spectrum we find an unbalanced person who has denied or repressed one of the processes involved: the Stalinist commissar has silenced his own conscience and repressed moral awareness (the 'saint' in himself), while the yogi denies the need for political action (the 'revolutionary' in himself). Koestler raises the question as to whether or not we can integrate the best of both processes *in ourselves*.

In practice we find that the most revolutionary or transformative aspects of our lives are those processes concerned with inner change and growth, connectedness, wholeness. As we have seen, this inner development involves increasing awareness of our power to change things in the world at large. The more we liberate our higher faculties, the more we come to see that we are nothing like as powerless as we thought we were. The political dimension is completely inseparable from the psychological and metaphysical.

Throughout the Christian centuries, a necessary part of the consolidation of ecclesiastical power was the metaphysical repression of the people and the maintenance of élitist and remote definitions of the saint, who had to be seen as a very special, rare and holy person who obeyed all the rules of mother Church, was elevated on a pedestal and enveloped in a cloud of pious religiosity.

When we cease dealing in stereotypes and externalized projections – 'saint' elevated on remote pedestal and 'revolutionary' making fiery speeches at the barricades – we begin to see that the liberation of our natural higher faculties (the saint in us) is a revolutionary process. In this deeper sense the saint is the revolutionary and the true revolutionary is the saint.

Contemplation and action

Koestler's commissar represents the ultimate extreme of political activism – action as an end in itself, action cut off from deeper roots. The western version of the yogi (the contemplative in his cell) symbolizes total political inertia and complete withdrawal from the world. Thus in an age when anything associated with contemplation is despised, the act of asserting our deeper needs and our right to silence is by its very nature revolutionary. If frenetic activity is the norm, to assert our more contemplative needs is bound to be revolutionary. If consumerism is the norm, to express our more creative faculties involves challenging currently prevailing values.

If one leads a life where one is constantly surrounded by noise, in the workplace and at home, silence seems like an élitist luxury. But the noise is drowning out a natural and necessary aspect of being. Fascist futurists such as Marinetti exalted and worshipped as a pseudo-religion the power and thrust of speed, noise and aggressive action. In this respect urban–industrial life today has developed in a direction which would have met with Marinetti's approval. Modern life quite frequently engulfs the human spirit in a great fascist tidal wave of noise and frenetic activity – an aggressive lifestyle highly conducive to the conduct of war. It is a sort of war in itself and is therefore reactionary rather than genuinely progressive.

When we just look quietly – which is what the word 'contemplation' means – we see that inner liberation is the most precious of all freedoms and inner bondage the worst of all prisons. 'Con-temple' means literally 'to make a temple with', to stake our claim to a timespace of stillness.

The choice in the popular mind seems clear-cut: either action man living in the real world, or monk living in a monastery withdrawn from the world. When contemplation is identified with a monastic form of quietism and withdrawal, while action is simply that which is not still or at rest, then the two seem to be mutually opposed. It is thus generally assumed that if you are leading an active life you are being the opposite of contemplative, and vice versa. Contemplation is seen as the opposite extreme of action.

As defined by the western Church, contemplation was reserved for a spiritual élite, being seen as a rare vocation suitable only for a few saintly people. A supernaturalist ecclesiastical ideology was projected onto what is in reality a natural process, thus effectively marginalizing it away from the sociopolitical mainstream of everyday life. Priests had to choose between the *vita activa* (parish work), or the *vita contemplativa* (a monastic community). The choice implied radical opposition between the two and contemplation was seen as something far too holy and exalted for ordinary mortals, something that took place in the cloistered stillness of a monastery well away from action in the bad old world.

The Reformation, industrial revolution and subsequent ascendancy of the protestant work ethic all contributed to the splitting away of contemplation, resulting in the now familiar caricature of a non-definition. The protestant work ethic defines work in visibilist terms and the implicit assumption is that whatever is not visible work cannot be true work. This visibilist definition of work ignores all the unseen work that goes on under the surface – the more subtle work of the psyche, the creative work of the imagination, the hard, sometimes painful, inner work. This sort of work does not conform to the narrow norms of industrial productivity, but it is still work.

The more action man is the role model, the more the need for stillness is repressed. Sometimes it is only when people suffer breakdowns that they re-examine the values they live by. Pressure of work is only one facet of a breakdown. Its deeper cause is metaphysical repression – denial of higher values and the need for periods of stillness. The result of looking quietly at what we are doing also entails a moral re-assessment of our motives. Once this process is under way, we have an internal revolution on our hands and a complete re-ordering of priorities.

New values

Currently prevailing monetarist values have created an unjust, unrepresentative society and we now need a new set of values that reflect more truly our deeper needs. When 'religion' and 'politics' are defined in narrow superficial terms and kept in their respective little compartments, no real connection can take place between higher values and activity in daily life. An apartheid policy of separate development applied to religion and politics entails denial of the essence of religion and repression of the moral aspect of politics.

In an article in *Resurgence*, Clive Ponting raises some questions that are fundamental to those seeking real change, but who are excluded from the centres of power and decision-making. The article is entitled 'Politics or Real Change?' The 'or' indicates a choice between politics as currently defined, or real change which might eventually alter the political structure. As a former civil servant in the Ministry of Defence, Ponting had first-hand experience of the self-validating nature of present-day politics: 'In practice the purpose of politics is to validate the existing system'. If the existing system is fundamentally unjust and unrepresentative (which it is), merely to validate it is clearly not the true role of politics. Many tend to shun 'politics' as a whole because they have lost sight of its true purpose – its reformative role. Since the absence of proportional representation keeps those who seek real change from power, we are left with a change in values:

> Values must change first and then we have to hope that this can in some way be articulated into the political and economic system . . . We need a set of values that reflect a more humane and dignified approach to life. Without that change there will be no lasting solution to the problems that beset us, only short-term political change. These values are not new; they have existed for centuries in true religious thought but have only rarely been applied.[2]

When politics confines itself only, or mainly, to *how* questions (how to keep inflation down) rather than *why* and *where* questions (why produce goods we don't need? where is economic growth leading us?), it removes itself from the moral core of life. So when people say that this 'politics' is irrelevant to real issues they are quite right, but they are referring to pseudo-politics, not the real thing. People have always asked politically awkward questions on the deeper motives of certain actions and they will go on asking such questions.

In the past this moral dimension was part and parcel of the political mainstream, as Edward Thompson stresses:

> Those working in the laboratories of the spirit and the mind took a central part in the nation's discourse. They also asked *why* and *where* questions. We're scarcely able to ask these questions in the central arena of politics today.[3]

It is within the subsoil of our own culture that we have to find the new perspectives and vision we so badly need today. Each person is a laboratory of the spirit, and life is a continuous experiment with time. The new set of values we need can only come from within ourselves and we are all rooted in the subsoil of a culture shaped by the judaeochristian tradition. This is why we see the world as we do and why we think as we do. It also determines the way we perceive the thought process. We cannot import some exotic oriental metaphysical cocktail and expect it to work miracles on 'The Western Condition'. Instead we have to rediscover the timeless and universal aspects of our own tradition and re-connect these to the rest of the world.

While it is a truism that we only see what we want to see, it is equally true that we can all see more clearly, gain more insight, be more aware, if we really want to enough. There is nothing exclusive or esoteric about this perfectly natural perceptual process. Seeing more clearly makes accessible to us a new level of being previously deemed to belong only to a sublime and exalted realm far beyond the reach of ordinary mortals.

The clarification of perception involves the recovery of our own natural visionary birthright – a faculty as natural as hearing or speaking. On seeing more clearly we see that we are all of us in one way or another bound up with this process of creative growth and inner liberation. We then cease to marginalize ourselves, disqualify ourselves from what has traditionally been seen as an exclusive little club of illuminati, a freemasonry of seers, saints and sages, an intellectual coterie of savants, writers and poets.

'We can never do justice to one another as social animals until we have each done justice to the visionary powers within us,' as Theodore Roszak so aptly puts it in *Where the Wasteland Ends*. He was writing during the heady days of the aftermath of 1968, in the cheerful expectation of an imminent 'epoch-making revolution in consciousness'. One might well wonder, over twenty years later, what could have happened to this particular revolution.

The market place has since become more ruthlessly competitive in our enterprise economy and the business world is more than ever detached from morality. Only when serious disasters occur – a ferry capsizing, a fire on an underground railway, a major explosion at an oil well – do people notice that profit comes first in the scale of monetarist values. The days when graffiti such as *l'imagination au pouvoir* and *soyez réalistes – demandez l'impossible* appeared on the walls of the Sorbonne now seem light years away. In 1982 (no, not 1892) a nation in Europe that usually likes to think of itself as quite reasonable, tolerant and civilized went to war with a state in South America. Despite all government attempts at disinformation, people later realized that young men had been killed and maimed in this, as in any other, war. It seems to be a case of *plus ça change, plus c'est la même chose*. Not exactly the stuff from which epoch-making revolutions in consciousness are made.

If we continue to define old concepts in old ways, we are unlikely to witness any substantial changes, let alone epoch-making revolutions in consciousness. If we think that an inner, invisible, silent revolution has to conform to the same old visibilist pattern in order to be regarded as real, then we are using outdated, traditional concepts of 'revolution'. These all belong to the old order and therefore define revolution in a reactionary way, which is somewhat contradictory.

Similarly if we identify a revolution in consciousness with a change in habitual thought patterns, we often find that we are still caught up in processes based on dualism and division. However revolutionary our *thinking* may be, the way we perceive the thought process remains reactionary if it is still bound up with the old order of time, which was for so many centuries of western history in effect war time – a notion of time that was highly conducive to the conduct of war and that gave the impression that war was a permanent feature of the human landscape.

Time and thought

The real revolution starts with a revolution in the perception of time and thought. In going beyond our old idea of time, we also go beyond our traditional perception of thought and the way we think we think, thereby opening up completely new, more globally appropriate vistas.

Conflict and war are part of the traditional temporal pattern – they have causes and effects. Higher values, peace, compassion and creative inspiration all belong to a different aspect of time. Eureka moments of inspiration do not occur as a result of thinking, but at times of perceptual clarity that are without apparent cause. The most ennobling and inspiring experiences transcend the narrow parameters of the conventional linear causal pattern; they are timeless.

When we see clearly, time and thought are not involved. Real insight involves instantaneous clarity of perception. So the inner revolution on which the outer revolution depends is more a question of seeing clearly than thinking differently. When we see clearly, we go beyond all the stale old dualisms and divisions which are the root of all conflict. When we really see, we see the oneness of life. With this vision war becomes completely impossible.

The inner essence of what all the great visionaries are referring to is in reality thoroughly accessible to us all. The way we perceive time is the key to understanding and relating to experiences hitherto kept well away from the activity of daily life. The language of religious experience can act as a barrier, but when we retranslate God language into ordinary time language we see more clearly what is actually happening under the dense and often obscure theological terminology. Religious preconceptions are no longer read into the experience and in this sense we see it in a more neutral and objective light. What is being described no longer seems so strange or supernatural, but quite normal and natural.

Access to the higher vision

According to Seyyed Hossein Nasr, a leading scholar of comparative religion, there is a lingua franca shared by virtually all religions concerning the perception of the present moment:

> The present . . . is the point where time and eternity meet; it symbolises hope and joy. It is the moment of faith and the door towards the non-temporal. . . Time itself is impregnated by the eternal in such a way that every moment of time is a gate to the eternal. . . Practically all the traditions of the world speak with the same tongue concerning the present moment, the instant, the present now, the eternal now. . . It is the now which all human beings experience at that moment which is their last earthly moment, namely the moment of death. The now is at once an anticipation of that moment and a going beyond it in the sense of experiencing an inner resurrection even before bodily death.[4]

This is the essence of religion – the anticipation in the present moment of the final moment and the transcendence of the final moment via an inner rebirth. This is the timeless core of the universal religion of humankind and it is in rediscovering this in ourselves and in our present historical situation that we rejoin the human family at a metaphysical level. The word 'religion' is from *religare*, to re-connect. We reconnect the idea of the eternal, which has acquired such otherworldly characteristics, with the time of *this* world and thereby restore a sense of the sacred to our present worldview. The same vision thus provides the basis for a sound ecology and a practical morality. We respect other people far more, because we see more clearly their own visionary potential.

Since the way we perceive time determines other perceptions, it follows that the renewal of religion and morality can only take place after initial clarification of the perception of time. It makes no sense to try and renew morality within the conventional order of time. Sooner or later, usually sooner, we find ourselves back in the old ways of thinking and therefore back in the old order of war time. Religious language, symbols and metaphors are responses to an initial perceptual experience that concerns the nature of time and its perceived connection with higher values that are timeless and universal. Time comes first; religion follows.

There is nothing élitist about the now; the present moment can hardly be regarded as remote and inaccessible. We may not wax lyrical or go into flights of mystical ecstasy about our own particular moments of illumination. We may or may not ascribe religious significance of any kind to them, depending on our definition of religion. We may simply prefer to hold our peace. But our silence should never be misconstrued as indicating that such wondrous things never happen.

It was the American philosopher, William James, who pioneered in an open-minded way the investigation of this aspect of human experience, free from either religious dogma or scientific reductionism. His classic work on the subject, *The Varieties of Religious Experience,* set the tone and opened the way to methodical inquiry in this field. In 1969 the marine biologist, Sir Alister Hardy, set up what was then called the Religious Experience Research Unit at Oxford, since renamed the Alister Hardy Research Centre.

For some years researchers associated with the centre have

been investigating experiences variously described as 'religious', 'mystical', 'transcendental', 'peak', 'ecstatic' and so on. Random surveys in both Britain and America indicate that something like 60% of both populations give positive responses when questioned on such phenomena.[5] The research centre's report for 1987 states that preliminary findings appear to overturn the widespread stereotype which has created the taboo on admitting such experiences. All the indications now are that people reporting transcendent experiences are most likely to be well educated, not suffering deprivation, happy, mentally well balanced, concerned about social justice and usually from a wide variety of religious and non-religious backgrounds.

People also commonly claim that such experiences have profoundly affected their lives, usually involving some of the following changes: fewer feelings of alienation from others and from the environment, an increase in the sense that life is meaningful, increased ability to cope with and survive crises, improvement in psychological balance, reduced dependence on material goods as a source of security, and increased concern for the good of others.

The research being done at the centre is now showing that, far from vanishing off the seemingly arid urban–industrial landscape, the visionary aspect of human experience is alive and well. The research also shows that peak experiences are certainly not restricted to any particular group of specially endowed people. On the contrary, to be more in touch with one's visionary faculties is an essential part of the definition of an integrated, normal person.

Many people find inner liberation not as a result of religious conversion, but after working their way through a painful phase of darkness and despair. This inner pilgrimage has been described in countless different ways in a rich variety of symbolic language since time immemorial. It is a journey that is universal, involving an encounter with images of light and darkness, angels and demons, heaven and hell, death and rebirth. For countless people life subsequently takes on a new, richer and deeper meaning. Things are never quite the same again.

In other words the revolution in consciousness, the perceptual transformation, is going on now, continuously, quietly, undramatically, unsensationally. It is not 'epoch-making' in the Hollywood hype sense, but it does provide the basis of a more globally appropriate worldview. The ending of visionary élitism entails the restoration of what is regarded as normal to a more balanced, more genuinely centred position.

In *The Perennial Philosophy*, Aldous Huxley observes that political policies rooted in the eternity philosophies – those belief systems that are not unduly obsessed with time – tend in practice to be tolerant and non-violent. This is because such philosophies are in turn based on the direct experience of inner liberation, awareness of the eternal now and rediscovery of the visionary aspect of life. Since this is a natural and normal part of life, the political process must be intimately concerned with metaphysical liberation.

A positive definition of peace

It is significant that Spinoza, who stands supreme for his spiritual vision of the world – he saw life 'under the form, or aspect, of eternity' – should also have been one of the very few western philosophers to have supplied a positive definition of peace. The relevant passage in his *Political Tract* reads as follows:

> A commonwealth whose subjects are restrained from revolting by fear must be said to be free from war rather than to enjoy peace. For peace is not the mere absence of war, but a virtue based on strength of mind.[6]

The original Latin for 'strength of mind' is *ex animi fortitudine,* which might also be translated as 'inner fortitude', 'inner strength', or 'soul strength'.

Spinoza was a visionary, a true philosopher in the original meaning of the word – a lover of wisdom, which of course entails heightened awareness of timeless values. Bertrand Russell, not always given to eulogizing his fellow philosophers, describes Spinoza as 'the noblest and most lovable of the great philosophers'.[7] He declined honours and earned his living as an optical craftsman, a grinder of lenses. This seems most appropriate, since his whole life was dedicated to the art of seeing clearly.

Instead of following the traditional line – that perception of the timeless in this world is something so abnormal and rare as not to merit serious consideration – Spinoza claims just the opposite. Namely, that the mystical vision, seeing this world in terms usually reserved for the hereafter, is the normal, natural and therefore correct way of perceiving the world. For a Jewish exile in Christian Europe in the seventeenth century this was, as far as the authorities of the day were concerned, about the most outrageous assertion imaginable. Not only was he promptly excommunicated from his own Jewish community in Amsterdam, but he was also condemned by orthodox Christian theologians from that day to this.

Spinoza was bound to be *persona non grata* to all religious establishments, because he stood for the kind of metaphysical liberation which churches have always claimed as their own exclusive monopoly. The reason why Russell admired him so much was that his pursuit of truth was both fearless and relentless – he took all his arguments to their logical conclusions, regardless of whether or not they were popular. What Christian theologians held against him was his pantheism, which in their eyes was heresy. Spinoza used the terms 'God' and 'nature' interchangeably (*Deus sive natura*) and saw no distinction between the natural world and the eternal. For him the ordinary everyday world was therefore sacred.

A person who sees this world as being in some sense sacred would be morally, psychologically and politically incapable of allowing such an infinitely precious world to be destroyed. On the contrary, such a person would treat it with enhanced reverence and respect. Increasing ecological concern and the green perception represent the renaissance, resurgence, rediscovery, of a vision similar to Spinoza's. Our concern for the environment in itself represents the restoration of a metaphysical dimension to our lives. There is certainly nothing new, least of all trendy, about this vision. It is timeless and therefore not subject to passing fads and fashions. Herein lies the deep strength of the vision.

Concern for the environment entails recovery of the timeless vision and this in turn provides the basis for a positive definition of the peace process. As a direct result of our ecological concern, we find that we have a new yet timeless worldview, as a result of which we take appropriate action at local level, or at least join one of the green pressure groups. We realize as part of our experience that the peace process is something very much more exciting and fulfilling than the old half-dead notion of mere absence of war.

There is no western equivalent of the Hindu concept of *ahimsa*. Because war time was the perceived norm for so many centuries, the best we can do is 'non-violence'. Soul strength and mere absence of violence are two very different things. We need a new language based on inner re-empowerment, a terminology that can touch the sacred timespace that dwells in each and every one of us, thus releasing hitherto largely untapped potential for creative growth and compassionate action.

It is globally inappropriate in these post-Hiroshima times that our lexicons and dictionaries should still give war pride of place and define peace in relation to it. *The Oxford English Dictionary*, for example, has ten columns on war, five on peace, the first of which reads: 'Peace 1. Freedom from, or cessation of, war or hostilities; that condition of a nation or community in which it is not at war with another'. In a well-known library in London there is a sign reading 'For peace, see war'.

Members of a society for so long dominated by the myth of the 'beast in man' did not believe they deserved real peace. Throughout the Christian centuries the idea of peace was more associated with the stillness of death than the activity of life. Peace was reified, turned into a static thing and projected away from this timeworld along with other higher values. It was seen as something that only began when life's action ended, thus inevitably acquiring a post-mortem stiffness. 'Rest in peace' assumes that there is peace in death, not life. Peace seemed to belong very much more to the next world rather than this one, because its time was not of this world. Those who claimed to experience the peace that passeth understanding and insisted on remaining alive to tell the tale were regarded with great suspicion by the ecclesiastical establishment. In a world seen as radically fallen and inherently sinful, war had to be the norm and peace therefore also had to be seen as too sublime, too good to be true, too otherworldly to be part of this world.

For centuries death was seen as the great liberator from this vale of tears and the Church stressed that it was in dying that one was born to eternal life. The American fundamentalists interpret this very literally and believe that the next world is a much better place than this one. When Nikita Khrushchev remarked that the west seemed in a great hurry to enter the next world (he was referring to the arms race), he put his finger on a raw nerve in the western psyche – the split timeworld outlook that had built up over the centuries and the manichaean view of the world which this entailed.

If the two timeworlds are not seen to connect or overlap in any way, peace is bound to retain its familiar post-mortem associations with the next world rather than this one.

The development of a positive philosophy of peace that defines strength primarily in moral, metaphysical terms rather than macho, physical terms is something all war departments could do without. As long as they can set the agenda by propagating the notion that strength is *solely* equated with physical force and armed might, then the war establishment appears to have a monopoly of *all* strength. In relation to this, peace is bound to appear weak, flabby, woolly, idealistic, wet, a surrender to superior strength, cowardice, lack of patriotism and so on.

The thought that peace might actually break out – the idea that a morally strong, positive, pacific process might actually get under way – is anathema to the war establishment. For those with a vested interest in maintaining the status quo, peace has to retain its otherworldly attributes, it has to stay very definitely outside and beyond the realm of the living, the real world.

John Rowan has suggested reversing the lexicographers' priorities, by re-defining war in relation to peace. Such a re-ordering of priorities might look something like this:

> Peace 1. A creative process where conflict is regulated and settled by non-violent means. Such means may include conflict resolution, mediation, conciliation, non-violent direct action, persuasion, graduated reciprocation in tension reduction, etc. Conflict may thus be avoided in the first place, or hostilities ended if already in existence.

> War 1. Absence of peace, particularly where hostilities have arisen on a large scale.[8]

The sociopolitical implications involved in the re-integration of the two timeworlds are immense in their transformative potential. The more familiar forms of liberation are meaningless if inwardly we remain oppressed, imprisoned. Metaphysical liberation and the development of soul strength are the most powerful forms of freedom. Nothing can prevail against them.

The forces of state oppression can deprive people of every other freedom but the deepest and most precious of all. There are numerous accounts of how people experience, usually to their own surprise, a form of metaphysical liberation while they are physically imprisoned. One political prisoner, for example, describes how he became convinced of the existence of an inner force that is empirically stronger than all outward forces of oppression:

> It is now an incontestable experience of life that in the depths of the human soul there dwells an unexplained force which is stronger – and not only symbolically, but empirically stronger – than all outward forces of oppression and destruction, however invincible they may seem. Those who describe these happenings, which have been repeated and confirmed hundreds of times under the most frightful conditions of imprisonment – have come to the conclusion that powerful forms of psychic energy are dormant in every human soul, that the psychic world cannot be separated from the physical, and that the thoughts and wishes of a person achieve far more in the outer physical world than do his hands.[9]

Imagine no pseudo-religion, imagine no pseudo-politics. There is a great wellspring of life-affirming pacific energy waiting to manifest itself. If we are discussing inner power (which we are), then we are discussing politics. Some activists still maintain the delusion that inner growth is irrelevant to politics. On the contrary, self knowledge and inner liberation form the basis of a more honest and relevant political process based on mutual respect and co-operation rather than puerile antagonisms, outdated childish confrontations and the same divisive mentality that underlies all conflict.

In the seventeenth century, Fr. Miguel de Molinos was sentenced to perpetual imprisonment by the Inquisition. His heinous crime was the grievous heresy of suggesting that contemplatives were justified in skipping some church rituals if they found these of no benefit to the spiritual life. As he was led away to his cell (where he spent nine years and then died) Molinos was overheard to remark that he was only being taken to his 'little retreat'. For him imprisonment was merely an extension of his already austere life of contemplation. He had experienced the kind of inner freedom no power on earth can remove or destroy. The forces of oppression, of all states and of all times, simply do not know how to handle this soul strength, this inner moral force which is universal and timeless.

Thomas Merton, who was a politically active contemplative, is addressing the poetic spirit in us all when he writes:

> Let us then recognize ourselves for who we are: dervishes mad with secret therapeutic love which cannot be bought or sold, and which the politician fears more than violent revolution, for violence changes nothing. But love changes everything.
>
> We are stronger than the bomb. [10]

III

SUSTAINABLE RELIGION

Our biblical tradition has conditioned us to think in terms
of beginnings, ends and linear causality. This is how we
perceive the world and the idea of experiencing a form of
time without any apparent beginning, end or causal line
usually strikes us as illogical if not inconceivable. Even when
we do become more aware of timeless moments, we still
find ourselves automatically asking, 'How long did it last?
When did it begin and end? What caused it?' So even on
those occasions when we perceive time differently from the
conventional version, we still tend to find ourselves superim-
posing chronological concepts that distort the underlying
nature of the event concerned.

Alternative perceptions

As we conduct our own experiments with time – by quietly
observing what is actually happening – we come to see the
difference between a culturally imposed concept and the
reality underlying it. We also come to see the difference
between a literal, final apocalyptic ending and a symbolic,
metaphorical 'death', the ending of a culturally determined
way of perceiving time.

The way we perceive time provides a, if not *the,* key to
the actual attainment of better times, a better world. The

multitude of horrors we are now faced with and all the many weapons of mass destruction, did not just appear at random out of the blue. To the extent that our particular western society is involved in destroying the natural environment and the production of these weapons, all such destructive processes represent the 'end products' of a specifically western worldview. The physical threats represent in concrete form underlying non-material, metaphysical processes. It is this metaphysical underpinning of our cultural worldview that needs to be changed before significant social and political changes can take place.

The green revolution and the peace process are indivisible. You cannot have one without the other. Clearly the peace process is not advanced if we continue to think in a manner conducive to conflict and war. Our political action is likely to continue to be divisive and alienating if it remains rooted in the same kind of dualistic outlook that underlies all conflict.

It is practically feasible to liberate ourselves from our own time conditioning. This is not some kind of fixed and unalterable 'law of human nature'. It is a culturally acquired notion or concept and therefore as much subject to change as any other. If other cultures at other times have succeeded in attaining the highest expressions of values and aesthetics as a result of alternative perceptions of time, there is no reason why ours should not do the same.

We have confused a myth, an idea, a concept, with fixed reality, 'human nature'. It is for this reason that we have hitherto only been able to define peace negatively in relation to war. As soon as we distinguish myth from reality, we obtain a more positive view of the peace process and our own human potential as an integral part of that process.

The cosmologies of other cultures do not display the same concern as ours with prime movers, cosmic architects or transcendent personal creators outside creation. There is certainly not the same obsession with linear causality. The people of other societies do not experience the same desire to set a beginning to the chain of events to which they belong. They are not particularly concerned about tracing origins and causes, nor do they divide past from present with the same rigidity as we do. The past co-exists with the present and the great mythical heroes live on in the continuous now.

The time language and symbolism of other cultures accept the paradoxical, both-and aspect of time: the horizontal time of everyday life and the vertical time of higher values. Other societies have a polychronic outlook: they accept as completely normal the coexistence of different orders of time. We have a monochronic view which is non-paradoxical, either/or, dualistic, separatist, fragmented. Polychronic time strikes the westerner as illogical: according to the narrow parameters of western logic, it cannot exist, therefore it does not. QED.

We need the humility to learn how those in other societies perceive us. A North American Indian, for example, describes his reaction to being taught to tell the time and work by the clock: 'I distrust anything I can't experience. I doubt its existence.' For him it seemed a very abstract idea to claim to be able to experience time in units of measurement according to the positions of the hands on a clockface:

> 'Abstractions mask reality. Abstractions mystify and confuse
> people so badly, they don't know when they are being
> robbed and enslaved. And they don't know when they are
> robbing and enslaving others . . . They are locked into
> timetables, locked into a system of living – and locked out
> of life'.[1]

In our culture, we describe a temporal abstraction as 'reality' and deny the reality of the very aspects of time that could endow our lives with deeper meaning. We use our temporal abstractions to close the window to the timeless, whereas the global norm throughout history has been to find ways and means of opening this window.

Now, however, the new physics and quantum theory are revealing every conceivable paradox in relation to time, which would seem to be everything except what we had always thought it to be. Our notion of time is undergoing radical reappraisals and the days of the western monochronic monopoly are numbered.

Clearly there is now a need to allow dualistic misperceptions to end, to 'die' a natural death, in order to make way for more integrated ways of perceiving the world. Pressure to conform to the conventional norm is strong. From long-standing habit and fear of social disapproval, we tend to dismiss as 'mere coincidences' the convergence in time of certain events which we might otherwise be able to see as meaningful, significant, or both.

Synchronicity

Jung coined the term 'synchronicity' for this process and traced the idea back to early Taoist origins. The subtitle of his essay on the subject is *An Acausal Connecting Principle.* [2] Synchronicity involves a meaningful convergence of outer and inner events that are not causally connected. In contrast with our western obsession with causality, the Chinese were more interested in finding out what likes to occur with what. We know from our own experiences that certain events seem to have 'personalities' of their own and seem to occur in a manner suggesting some kind of mutual compatability. We also know, in an intuitive way, when the time is right, or when the time is out of joint, 'out of sync'.

This more flexible and imaginative view of time allows us to re-open the window to the timeless, thereby re-connecting timeworlds usually seen as being completely separate. Such perceptions are, as we have seen, often accompanied by enhanced awareness of inner liberation, greater compassion and a strong sense of unity with the world as a whole.

In denying beforehand even the possibility of any such

process, we deprive our lives of deeper meaning and value, severing any connection with a greater form of time beyond the micro-time of everyday life – a time with no beginning, end or linear causal chain. We thereby deny ourselves the most precious of all freedoms – inner liberation and freedom from our own cultural conditioning.

For the process of inner growth and development to get under way and connect with sociopolitical life, we need new time models. We must also make use of available symbols and metaphors on the timeless perennial theme of death and rebirth.

Post-Hiroshima time

Our calendar is very accommodating about wars. It is the chronology of war time, giving the impression that wars come and go, always have and always will. But our calendar cannot accommodate the threat of omnicide, for the simple reason that omnicide is not war. Our calendar gives the false impression that nuclear omnicide is like any other war, except a bit bigger than usual.

The Gregorian calendar we take so completely for granted has only been in use for just over four centuries. It was originally introduced by Pope Gregory XIII in 1582, in order to determine the correct dates for religious holy days. It was devised in an era of certainty, in the sure belief that business would carry on as usual into the indefinite future. Empires and dynasties would rise and fall, war, plague, flood and pestilence would come and go, but the liturgical year and holy days of the church calendar would go on and on until the day of judgement.

The trouble with a calendar designed to convey the impression that business carries on as usual is that war business tends to be included on the agenda as well. For many centuries it was assumed that nation-states would settle their differences on the battlefield. War was seen as an extension of politics by other means.

If we now had to devise a new calendar that reflected our age more honestly, we would certainly not choose the Gregorian version. It belongs to the old order of pre-Hiroshima time, which entailed a mentality conducive to the conduct of war. From the dawn of human history, people had to live with the prospect of individual death. But since Hiroshima we have all had to live with the prospect of universal death, omnicide. There is no event in the whole of human history of comparable magnitude and 6 August 1945 marks the most radical of all divisions in history. Our present calendar completely fails to reflect this fact.

Arthur Koestler was one of the first to advocate the use of an alternative calendar, to put things in their correct chronological perspective. Writing in 1960, he suggested using 1945 as the year zero, thus making the year 1960 the year 15 pH new time (where p stands for post and H for Hiroshima.) [3] He conceded that there would be a period of incubation, since the unconscious has its own clock and its own way of adapting to what the conscious mind might reject as unacceptable. However, Koestler believed that recognition of the deeper implications of Hiroshima would gradually percolate into the collective psyche and in due course transform our whole outlook.

When we apply the pH calendar to the present and extend it to the year 2,000, it looks like this:

AD	pH
1990	45
1991	46
1992	47
1993	48
1994	49
1995	50
1996	51

1997	52
1998	53
1999	54
2000	55

Compared to the many millennia preceding Hiroshima, the few decades of post-Hiroshima time are insignificant. 'We are living between a death and a difficult birth', as Samuel Beckett aptly puts it. Nuclear deterrent strategy represents a refusal to accept the ending of the old order, the 'death' of war time. This refusal to accept a metaphorical death makes a literal one more likely. The strategists are like Rip van Winkle, having gone to sleep in an age when war could still be fought out between combatants without endangering civilian populations, let alone the whole species and its future. They have yet to wake up to the reality of the age of omnicide.

Crisis and opportunity

The crisis of the nuclear age is continuous. At any moment there could be another Chernobyl or something much worse. Just as we now live in an age of continual crisis, so we also live in an age of continual opportunity. Just as every moment of time is potentially critical, so it also represents an ever-present, ever-renewed opportunity to see what is really happening, to see in a way that would instantly make any thought of war utterly inconceivable.

According to conventional chronology, Hiroshima represents a somewhat bigger bang than usual on the battle graph of history. Theoretically this event should fade further and further into the past with the passage of time. It should become more detached from the present and those living in the world today. There should be less and less perceived connection between those who lived and died in that faraway Japanese city forty-five years ago and those living in western

Europe in the early nineties. New generations have since been born, Hiroshima has been rebuilt and business would appear to be carrying on as usual.

While there is a natural and healthy sense in which life has to carry on as usual even after the most terrible disasters, in this particular case time does not appear to be conforming to the conventional pattern. This particular wound to the human psyche seems actually to become more raw and exposed as each year passes. Rather than moving further away from those who suffered and died in Hiroshima and Nagasaki, there is a real sense in which we feel we are growing closer to them.

Under conventional pre-Hiroshima circumstances, we would hope and expect to see the mushroom-shaped cloud growing ever-fainter until it eventually disappeared over the horizon. But this event is failing to conform to the conventional western time model. The familiar shape of the sinister cloud is growing more clearly defined, as we become increasingly aware of the full extent of the dangers now faced by the whole planet and all its inhabitants.

We have no conceptual framework, no language, certainly no adequate concept of time, that come anywhere near helping us cope with the reality of our present age. We have never, ever, been here before and like the survivors of Hiroshima and Nagasaki, we too have lost the familiar bearings of the old order. We would rather worry about anything under the sun than face up to this, the most disturbing fact of our age.

If we decide not to indulge in all the many different forms of displacement and to face the threat of omnicide for what it actually is, we see that Hiroshima raises the most fundamental questions regarding chronology and the way we perceive time and history.

The ending of the old order

The business-as-usual school would concede that 6 August marks a new chapter in human history, the main text remaining unchanged. It is a very different matter to acknowledge that Hiroshima marks the ending of the whole book: that since August 1945 we have been living beyond our own historical process, beyond the old Genesis-Apocalypse timeline, beyond our biblical cosmology, beyond our old dualistic ways of thinking that gave the impression that war was an inevitable and permanent part of the human condition.

Deeply ingrained in the western psyche is the idea that our history unfolds within the Genesis-Apocalypse linear model. It requires a major perceptual shift to accept the possibility that we might be living outside this model, beyond our own timeline. We can see Hiroshima in terms of a prototype of the actual Apocalypse, thus enabling us to think in a post-apocalyptic way. So although the actual risk of a nuclear apocalypse is part of present reality, there is a sense in which we need to acknowledge that a metaphysical apocalypse has already taken place, totally shattering the mind sets that propped up the old order.

Hiroshima provides an opportunity to end ways of thinking that could engulf the whole world in omnicide. In order to avoid or prevent an actual Apocalypse, we have to be able to look beyond a metaphorical one. If we are willing to take this opportunity, undergoing radical shifts in perception, undertaking our own experiments with time, we find completely new vistas opening up before us, completely new ways of seeing the world.

Claude Lanzmann, producer of the epic film *Shoah,* argues that the shattering of chronology is an essential safeguard against any repetition of Auschwitz. If this applies to the genocide of the holocaust, it applies all the more to the potential omnicide represented by over a million possible Hiroshimas. The wound of Auschwitz has to remain raw in

the Jewish psyche. The wound of Hiroshima has to remain
raw in the global human psyche, in the consciousness of each
and every person.

In *A Planet to Heal*, Pedro Arrupe, who was living near
Hiroshima at the time of the explosion, describes what the
initial blast did to his wall clock: it stopped it. This seemed
an accurate symbolic expression of what had actually happened. On the morning of that day, at exactly that time, the
old order died and a new era was born. What happened bore
no relation to the ordinary notion of time:

> That silent and motionless clock has become a symbol. The
> explosion of the first atomic bomb has become a para-
> historical phenomenon. It is not a memory; it is a perpetual
> experience, outside history, which does not pass with the
> ticking of the clock. . . It has no relation to time.[4]

Largely as a result of the resurgence of the peace movement
in the early eighties, we are now far better informed about
the nuclear situation. We are now beginning to see that,
underlying the terrible images evoked by the word 'Hiroshima', there are some profound philosophical issues. The
image of the clock of western history stopping at the moment
of detonation brings many awkward paradoxes to the surface
of consciousness. Now we are all philosophers, in the sense
that we all face the deepest issues of life and death, being and
nothingness, issues that were previously seen as the exclusive
preserve of an élitist group of academics. Today we all have
an equal right to speculate on the most profound metaphysical issues – a duty, not just a right. The cosy little world
of philosophy has also been 'blown apart' metaphorically and
each and every one of us has the same need, if not obligation,
to make what sense we can of our present predicament.

The survivors of Hiroshima and Nagasaki are known as
hibakusha, which means literally 'explosion-affected', or
'death-immersed'. The *hibakusha* know from their own
experience what it feels like to have all bearings, markers,

signposts, blown away. They know about no-thing, no-self
– the lack of any definition of self. They know what it is for
their time to come to an end, to die in every sense but
physically, yet to go on existing beyond all the familiar old
temporal and historical landmarks. The *hibakusha* experience
the continuous paradox of living beyond their own historical
process: their whole world ended, yet they go on living.
There is no historical precedent for life after history. There
is no philosophy that comes anywhere near doing justice to
the truth of this situation, other than the philosophy of going
beyond philosophy.

In his study of post-Hiroshima theology, Jim Garrison
stresses that there is a real sense in which we are all of us
hibakusha:

> Just as all Japanese, whether officially *hibakusha* or not,
> suffered the impact of the atomic bomb experience,
> particularly the youth, so all of us are in some degree affected
> as well; that is to say, that the psychological occurrences in
> Hiroshima and Nagasaki have an important bearing on all
> of human existence.[5]

Now we are all of us *hibakusha*, in every sense but the literal –
metaphysically, spiritually, psychologically, philosophically
and morally.

Just as 'never again Auschwitz' involves breaking down
the conventional time barriers between past and present, so
'no more Hiroshimas' entails an even more radical break
with the old order of time. As honorary *hibakusha,* we all
share with the official *hibakusha* the same supreme paradox
of living beyond our own timeworld. As Garrison puts it,
'By exploding the normal cyclic patterns through which the
human family is accustomed to live and to die, the atom
bomb placed us all in an altered state of space-time . . . The
"end of time" is now an omnipresent reality.'

This really does seem like 'the end of the world' to a
monochronic culture like ours. To face the prospect of the

end of time as an omnipresent reality is, to say the least, somewhat daunting to a culture that has reduced the whole temporal process to such a narrow linear model. We are taught to think non-paradoxically: if we've reached the end of the line, then that's it. *Finito*. For the nuclear powerbrokers it is as if the prospect of a metaphorical, figurative, symbolic ending can only be expressed literally, physically. They equate a symbolic death with an actual one. All their bombs represent an obsessive attachment to the old order, the rigid and inflexible military mind.

The more rigid and inflexible our view of time, the harder we find it to accommodate new perceptions, alternative time vistas, and the more difficult we find it to live with the omnipresent reality of the end of time. Our time conditioning has the effect of repressing alternative perceptions that fail to fit into the narrow reductionist model. Yet in facing and accepting a metaphorical ending, a symbolic death, we make a literal ending – an actual death in its omnicidal, universal form – less likely.

To this day, the *hibakusha* refer to the bomb that was dropped on Hiroshima as the Christian bomb. This is exactly what it was: the product of a culture shaped by Christian values and its use was sanctioned by those claiming to be fighting in defence of Christian civilization. Yet in reality it marked the demise of triumphalist Christianity. The Christian bomb marked the end of something that had until then been seen as an essential part of western history: the time of crusaders and *conquistadores,* the time of arrogant missionaries, the macho-aggressive time of imperial domination, the time of 'Onward Christian Soldiers'. Now the Christian soldiers could march no further, except over the abyss. All the old assumptions were blown sky high with the Christian bomb, especially such notions as a 'just war'.

We can now see more clearly that Hiroshima has to mark the end of the road for those triumphalist attitudes that provided justification for wars down through the Christian centuries and which still fuel the arms trade. If we are serious about actually ending this death industry, we have to look into its inner causal functioning, not just react to external events as they occur. The old order of Christian time belonged to an arrogant culture that ruthlessly eliminated whole societies in the name of Christian civilization and Manifest Destiny. This war time has to be allowed to die a natural death so as to make way for more globally appropriate perceptions, ways of seeing that are more conducive to human and ecological survival.

The death and rebirth of Christian time

Christian time was hoist with its own petard at Hiroshima. The new chronology provides an opportunity for western religion to 'die' to itself, liberate itself from its dualistic, split time outlook, thus allowing the demise of war time to take place at a deep level in the western psyche. Moral condemnation of war has never brought about the abolition of war and it never will as long as it originates in ways of thinking rooted in the old order, where war time is the perceived norm. War can only be abolished when the time, causality and ways of thinking conducive to war are first brought to an end.

Using the alternative post-Hiroshima calendar does not entail denying that the pre-Hiroshima Christian centuries ever took place. We are all part of that history, no matter what sort of calendar we may in future devise in order to do greater justice to our present age. The Hiroshima calendar provides an opportunity to make a fresh psychological start, a fresh start in our modes of perception.

The death-rebirth theme is deeply embedded in our cultural mythology. The whole idea of allowing certain processes to die so that more creative ones can come into being is the very essence of religion itself. It is a liberating process, whereby we re-connect with the timeless and universal aspect

of religion. It is a metaphor for growth, expressed throughout human history in a rich variety of cultural symbolism.
It is perhaps the most ancient of myths, the most rooted in
mother earth herself, the most natural of processes. For
growth to occur – whether individual or social – that which
is already deathly, stiff, corpse-like, needs to be allowed to
die so that more vital, creative and life-affirming processes
can come into being, grow and develop.

All the main religious traditions, especially Buddhism,
have always stressed the importance of non-attachment. The
death-rebirth process involves this letting go, release, liberation, ending. Until late medieval times, Christianity used
to teach the craft of dying. The idea was to cultivate in life
the sort of non-attachment represented by death. Properly
understood, this entailed a healthy approach to death itself,
because one was already inwardly free. This is the meaning
of the saying that it is in learning how to die that one truly
learns how to live. It involves a willingness to let go inwardly
of everything, not only material possessions, but also concepts, ideas and beliefs – the goods and chattels of the mind.
These are usually the hardest to part with.

In *The Turning Point,* Fritjof Capra writes that the experiential encounter with birth and death often amounts to a true
existential crisis, forcing people to re-examine their lives
and the values they live by. Worldly ambitions, competitive
drives, the longing for status, power or material possessions
'all tend to fade away when viewed against the background
of potentially imminent death'.[6]

Until Hiroshima, the background of potentially imminent
death was something we only faced individually. Now we all
face it collectively, socially, globally. The world macrocosm
faces the existential crisis as one individual microcosm and
vice versa. Never has the need for more awareness of inner-
outer connections been greater than it is now. One has only
to imagine the socially transformative effects of collectively
facing up to our existential crisis and the way this results in

a re-examination of the meaning of our lives and the values we live by.

Christian time reborn is a more balanced time. It is no longer biased in a macho-aggressive direction, but recovers its own suppressed and repressed feminine characteristics. It is thus a more natural time, in greater harmony with the overwhelming majority of other cultural worldviews. Throughout the pre-Hiroshima Christian centuries, the western notion of time set us apart from the rest of the world and now threatens to blow the whole world apart, or poison it more gradually. The demise of this war time and the rebirth, or recovery, of a more globally appropriate time, re-connects our western culture to humanity as a whole and to its storehouse of timeless wisdom and mythology, thus allowing us to rediscover our own sacred roots in the soil of mother earth herself.

The green myth

We have long ago moved out of the structurally rigid mythology of traditional Christianity. The inner meaning is now seen to be more symbolic than literal, but no less valid for this. The underlying rites of passage and psychological phases remain true and retain their perennial, timeless quality.

In *The Politics of Hope*,[7] Trevor Blackwell and Jeremy Seabrook show the main mythic phases in western history: from traditional Christian myth, via the submyths of capitalism and socialism, to the green myth. Each phase goes through parallel versions of the original Christian myth: initial state of innocence, fall, wanderings in the wilderness, redemptive sacrifice, resurrection, day of judgement, heaven and hell. The authors rightly stress that the green myth is not new to the world; it draws on themes and structures which are part of the mythic storehouse of humankind.

The green myth is where we are now. It represents in symbolic form our actual present reality. As we see our own present time more clearly, we also see that the green myth differs from the Christian myth in several major respects.

Instead of regarding the fall as irreversible, it expresses the idea that to live in a state of balance with nature is our true, natural and permanent condition. The green version of the fall is represented by unsustainable religion, leading to unsustainable ways of living and unsustainable economies. This is the contemporary green fall which it is our duty to reverse. It is, as we have seen, a case of rediscovering our true selves rather than inventing or concocting some completely new myth. The concept of linear time and the idea of an irreversible state of original sin militate against this recovery of our true and natural state.

Just as the green myth expresses faith in our ability to recover our original blessing, it also expresses faith in our ability to prevent our own end. It is based on the view that the Apocalypse can be avoided by human effort, that a final ending of the human story can be prevented by our own insight and action. This represents the exact opposite of the grim determinism of biblical fundamentalism, which holds that a nuclear Apocalypse is part of the divine plan and that humans therefore have no business interfering with this pre-ordained scenario. The psychologically disempowering effects of this manichaean pessimism run deep and extend far beyond those who would describe themselves as fundamentalists (who are very few in number). The amount of positive, pacific and healing energy that is locked up as a direct result of the view that the individual can do absolutely nothing about the state of the world is incalculable. It is so incalculable that we hardly dare to imagine the benign sociopolitical effects of liberating such energy. An essential part of the green myth is faith in our ability to recover those higher values that were traditionally held to belong only to the next world.

Conventional politics in this country remain based on mythologies that are no longer appropriate to global reality.

Central to all the sub-myths of the parties of the old order is the illogical and unnatural idea of never-ending economic growth. This is a major myth in its own right, an article of faith, a pseudo-religion. As Walter Schwarz puts it, 'Belief in universal economic growth at exponential rates of increase is a faith. There is nothing rational about it: indeed it is demonstrably irrational. It is unnatural for a start. Healthy living things grow to maturity and then stop growing.' Schwarz goes on to say:

> Faith means putting an absolute value on something you believe in. A nature-friendly faith has to start with a loss of faith in economic growth, preferring spiritual growth and community values. . . Burning rainforest is wicked by this faith, as it is for Indians being smoked out of their Amazonian culture. Such a faith is needed in the West, to replace the 'growth' model for the rest of the world. It is held among Christians, but more often among green-minded people I would call post-Christians. They have no dogma other than believing in nature.[8]

The green political agenda has sought to apply the word 'sustainable' to just about everything except religion. It is when we turn to spiritual matters that we are faced with what Charlene Spretnak calls 'a huge hole in Green politics'. She then asks the key question: 'What is sustainable religion?'[9]

It is certainly easier to define sustainable religion negatively rather than positively. We have a clearer idea of what it is not than of what it is. It is not anthropocentric, rejecting the human-centred orientation of humanism and those New Age theories that place humans rather than nature at the centre of things. It rejects the mechanistic soullessness of modernism – rootless urbanism, nationalistic chauvinism and sterile secularism. It vigorously rejects patriarchal values, not only male domination but the wider historical accretions of a patriarchal culture: love of hierarchical structures and competition, either/or modes of relating (either dominance or submission), alienation from nature and suppression of feelings. It rejects all this and much more, but such rejection does not in itself tell us just what sustainable religion is.

Sustainable religion is like the clear fresh water of a mountain stream that flows from the most natural source of being. It is the life-affirming joy of the morning chorus on a spring day. It is compassion. It is the peace we experience in moments of silent contemplation. It is recognition of the divine within nature (our own natures as well as nature as a whole) and the respect that is its due. It is accessible to all. It is ecocentric rather than egocentric.

The green myth entails a more inspiring vision of who we really are, accepting our shadow elements and limitations, but also recognizing our higher potential, our ability to experience the mystical ecstasy of the saints. We all share the need to perceive a deeper meaning to life beyond purely materialistic values, the need to realize – make real – our natural higher potential.

The phoney advertising images of the capitalist-consumerist sub-myth are based on the unquestioned assumption that absolutely everybody is striving for purely materialistic goals. No adman would dare to whisper a hint of spiritual questioning, moral doubt or metaphysical speculation. We do not see pictures of people leading the good life, people who have made it and have everything they could possibly wish for, with the caption 'What next?' It is tacitly assumed that if you do not yet own a yacht moored at Monte Carlo, this is what you want and when you've got one yacht, you will of course want two. . . But sometimes those who have made it find that their Dynasty-style homes are built in a spiritually arid desert.

It is now becoming increasingly obvious to those living in unsustainable consumerist economies that the less habitable the planet becomes, the fewer the number of people who will be able to lead even the most basic existence. The well-being of the planet is not seen as the most urgent priority issue to those in desperate need, especially when isolated ecological issues are presented in a disjointed way. The homeless in 'cardboard city', those waiting years in the queue for surgery, single parents struggling in situations of acute deprivation to rear young children, old people living in fear and isolation on bleak housing estates – all are fellow members of our own species who lack basic needs. They need more than lectures on the plight of whales, or theories about Gaia. They need better housing, more resources in the health service, more support, more caring, more warmth.

The most effective way to reconnect person and planet, to recover a more integrated perception of the world and one's place in it, is to stress more robustly the paramount nature of universal values. In order to liberate the energy attached to the higher values, which is at present locked up, denied, repressed, we need a philosophy of re-empowerment based on recovery of our true potential as healers and peacemakers.

By its very nature, the peace process takes us into the realm of higher values which transcend all the labels we try to stick on ourselves. Such values also transcend national boundaries, cultural and religious traditions. They possess us, we do not possess them. There is no monopoly of any kind on such values, which are the soul of the world. Different cultures and civilizations come and go, but the natural core remains. The more any particular expression of spirituality is in harmony with the world-soul, the more it expresses a sustainable form of religion.

The recovery of timeless values

Perhaps the most liberating perception or insight for those living in a predominantly transcendentalist judeochristian cultural tradition is the realization that timeless values, previously seen as belonging only to some hypothetical 'next world', in reality belong to this world. In this sense, pantheistic humanism represents a deeply spiritual process: the reclamation of higher values previously perceived as belonging to another world, another place, another time. Pantheistic humanism reinstates the divine in the soul of the world and therefore in our souls too.

In rejecting the traditional dualistic division between the natural and the supernatural, one is reclaiming timeless values for this world and thereby immeasurably enriching our perception of the world and those living in it. The old image of the remote God the Father inevitably diverted attention away from what the Quakers call 'that of God in every person'. It is precisely because Quakers believe in this indwelling divine Spirit that they have been so consistent in their opposition to war.

We now need to reassess philosophies that have been overlooked as a result of theological prejudice. One such is the philosophy of Ludwig Feuerbach, a visionary who dedicated his life to the liberation of inner potential and the reclamation of higher values. He was convinced that the major obstacle to human happiness was the divided consciousness, the propensity that humans suffer from to compartmentalize their interior lives so that they remain blind to their true potential.[10]

Feuerbach was born in 1804 and died in 1872. He studied under Hegel in Berlin and later became the leading Hegelian heretic, turning idealist philosophy on its head. As Kamenka puts it, 'To the young radicals of Germany, including Marx and Engels, Feuerbach was the man who had overcome the Hegelian system, who had restored man's alienated essence to man, who had pointed the way to true social and political liberation.'[11]

In these post-Hiroshima times, sustainable religion entails a similar willingness to turn conventional wisdom upside down and subject our most cherished beliefs and assumptions to the crucible of the age. It is this willingness to turn things upside down, see the world in a completely new light, that is important, not the detailed aspects of any particular philosophy. If this perceptual change was necessary in Feuerbach's time – in order to reclaim human potential in the face of metaphysically repressive doctrines – it is clearly all the more necessary today in the face of total repression of the human spirit under the threat of omnicide.

In his first major work, *Thoughts on Death and Immortality*, Feuerbach argued that traditional theology was responsible for blocking, repressing or distorting the perceived value of human life in this world by focusing so much spiritual energy on the idea of the immortality of the soul in the next life. He believed that this projection or transference of higher values away from this world into some future hypothetical post-mortem world inevitably had the effect of alienating us from our own true inner essence.

When the book first appeared in 1830 it caused outrage in official circles and ensured the author's exclusion from a professional academic career – something he did not find particularly tragic. Feuerbach was a completely independent thinker and made it clear that he found more insight with nature and country people than with the academics of the day: 'The sand which Berlin's State philosophy threw into my eyes I wash out completely with the spring of nature. I learnt logic at a German university, but optics, the art of *seeing*, I learnt for the first time in a German village. The philosopher, at least as I understand him, must have nature as his friend, he must know her not only from books but face to face.'[12]

Just as he had reversed Hegel's idealist philosophy, so Feuerbach maintained that the old theological view of the next world is in reality a misplaced or unrealized perception of this world. Like Spinoza, from whom he drew much inspiration, he was a pantheist and perceived the divine presence throughout the natural world: 'Know love and you have known God. . . Thus only the genuine pantheist knows what love is; only he can love. Apart from pantheism everything is egoism, self-seeking, vanity, greed, mercenariness, idolatry.'[13]

Feuerbach held that symbolic 'little deaths' within life are what give life deeper meaning and significance. In the self-giving of love, for example, personal and transpersonal, temporal and timeless aspects are united. This entails a 'little death' of the timebound ego, a letting go, release, liberation – all symbolizing the non-attachment entailed in actual death.

The ending of a person's life is an integral part of the definition of that life. The notion of the soul marching on through the next world in a purely linear way completely distorts perception of the soul in this life. If a table, for example, had no outer edge or boundary, it would cease to be a table. Similarly the outer edge or boundary of a given person's life are an integral part of the definition of that life. Feuerbach held that, far from making life meaningless, the physical reality of death is precisely what gives it meaning: 'Death is the presupposed and preceding condition of your existence. As you depart from existence in death, so you enter existence only in death. Is not the end of something always its true beginning? Do you not obtain the concept of something only at its end? Do you not perceive its essence only when it ceases?'[14]

Feuerbach's *Essence of Christianity* appeared in 1841, caused a sensation and sealed his radical reputation. He subsequently devoted much of his time to the defence of his position, pointing out that the book had never been intended as an attack against religion as such, but that it was an attempt to liberate the moral content of religion and clarify perception of its inner essence. By no means for the first or last time, a great liberator of the human spirit was branded as a destructive atheist, or even a blasphemer. Feuerbach retained this destructive, reductionist image from that day to this and was confined to a no man's land somewhere between theology and philosophy. Theologians still tend to see him as the arch-enemy of Christian doctrine, as the one responsible for the most devastating demolition job ever undertaken on Christian theology. Philosophers tend to regard him as a theologian. But as we have observed, he saw himself as a philosopher and a reappraisal of his philosophy is long overdue. It throws much light on our present age and provides many useful metaphors, in particular with regard to non-attachment and the willingness to part with our favourite prejudices.

Another liberator of the inner essence of religion was Krishnamurti. Born in 1895 and brought up in a brahmin family, Jiddu Krishnamurti was spotted by Annie Besant and her theosophical colleagues, who believed that he was destined to be the new Messiah. The boy was taken away from his family and groomed for his future messianic rôle. In 1911 Mrs Besant founded the Order of the Star in the East, with Krishnamurti as its head. Its members were convinced that a new coming was imminent. Psychologically the idea of a second coming from the east fitted in perfectly with the perceived needs of a very large number of people at the time.

Krishnamurti began to travel round the world, addressing ever larger audiences. However, as time went on it gradually dawned on his followers that he was no longer saying the comforting things they expected to hear. In fact he was beginning to say some rather disturbing things. This all came to a head in 1929, when he dissolved the Order of the Star and declared that he did not want followers, that truth was 'a pathless land' and that his sole concern was to set people psychologically free, especially from all spiritual authority.

Krishnamurti's story is a metaphor of power: what to do with the power others transfer or project onto a messianic figure, how to reclaim and realize that power for ourselves. It is unusual, to say the least, for somebody at the receiving end of a massive amount of messianic projection to totally reject such projection and 'throw it back' at those doing the projecting. But this is precisely what Krishnamurti did, uncompromisingly, until the day he died.

Either implicitly or explicitly, the perception of time is the main theme running through his life's work. He realized that time is the key to all other perceptions: clarify the perception of time and all else will be seen much more clearly. This is certainly the dominant theme of the dialogues between Krishnamurti and the physicist, David Bohm, appropriately entitled *The Ending of Time*.[15]

The main argument can be briefly summarized as follows. The ego is bound up with dualistic, fragmentary thought. Time and thought replicate each other so closely that, perceptually, they merge into a single process. Thought is time, in the linear-successional sense ('one damn thing after another'). The way we think determines the way we think about time and the way we perceive time determines the way we think. So if we are really serious about wanting to liberate ourselves from our own timethought conditioning and see clearly, we are bound to ask the key question posed by Krishnamurti: can we end our own psychological time, go beyond the old fragmentary, dualistic timethought process and actually experience true inner freedom? This is the key question of our age.

The actual act of asking the right question involves us in a timeless process pre-existing the posing of the question. Merely by asking the right questions, we gain admission to the universal perennial philosophy of humankind, which has no beginning, no end, certainly no final solution, no nice, neat, non-paradoxical, either/or answer. The right question expresses the universal need for higher values. Simply to express this need is in itself a liberating experience which somehow seems to clarify our perception of those values, thus making them more accessible.

To assert that truth is a pathless land is another way of saying that there is no such thing as a magic system waiting to be discovered. All methods, techniques and systems involve timethought: it is assumed that the beginner starts at the beginning and that if she/he perseveres, she/he will advance progressively up the learning ladder towards some form of enlightenment at the top. People take this school model so much for granted that they tend to get quite thrown out when it is suggested that there may not be any models of any kind.

Einstein's truism that the splitting of the atom has changed everything except the way we think has become a mantra, monotonously repeated as though the act of repetition involves some kind of magic formula, some occult power of transmutation. But before being able to really change any-thing, we surely need a reasonably clear idea of what has to be changed. To retain the computer model of the brain and equate this with all our mental processes simply involves inserting a different programme into the same machine. In order to undergo a real change, we first have to discard completely this or any other model of the mind. To think differently while continuing in the same old dualistic time-thought mode is only a cosmetic change, not a change going right down into the deepest levels of being where there are no models of any kind.

To see really clearly is to change. When we look with concentrated attention at what is actually going on in the present, we instantly liberate ourselves from our own past conditioning. This is real change, the change of true inner freedom.

In seeing that there is no journey from here to there, we also see that no time is involved: we have always been, are now and always will be 'there'. From this position we also see that peace and love are both causeless – they do not belong to the same old dualistic time model which is at the root of all conflict. This is the essence of sustainable religion: it is uncontrived, cannot be set up or programmed. It is spontaneous and no timethought is involved. So there is no question of asking how we get there. It is more a matter of seeing that we are there already.

We are the world

There is a sense in which a particular person at a particular time and place represents all persons of all times and places. The inner world microcosm is also the outer world macrocosm – a theme explored by Krishnamurti in *You are the World:* 'In oneself lies the whole world and if you know how to look and learn, then the door is there and the key is in your hand. Nobody on earth can give you that key or open that door except yourself.'[16]

The key is non-attachment, a willingness to let go all prior assumptions and prejudices. We are then in a position to become more aware of something beyond timethought that is timeless and incorruptible. In order to perceive this, 'The mind must be completely, totally still, which means time comes to an end; and in that there must be complete freedom from all prejudice, opinion, judgement. . . Then only one comes upon this extraordinary thing that is timeless and the very essence of compassion.'[17]

When we see more clearly, it seems as if we had been asleep before. Thomas Merton, for example, describes how he suddenly saw more clearly in this deeper sense while on a routine shopping expedition in his local town: 'In Louisville, at the corner of Fourth and Walnut, in the centre of the shopping district, I was suddenly overwhelmed with the realization that I loved all those people, that they were mine and I theirs, that we could not be alien to one another, even though we were total strangers. It was like waking from a dream of separateness.'[18]

When we wake up from the dream of separateness, we actually obtain a clearer perception of reality. But we generally tend to regard the dream as reality and the waking state as some very rare and special form of higher consciousness.

Merton felt that at that moment he obtained a clearer view of the actual human condition: 'It was as if I suddenly saw the secret beauty of their hearts, the core of their reality.' He believed that there was what he described as 'a point of nothingness and absolute poverty' at the centre of our being.

This state of inner non-attachment and freedom represents our actual human reality, but most of us spend most of our lives trying to fill our inner timespaces with every conceivable sort of mental furniture. When we die, we leave the whole lot behind – not only our material goods and chattels, but also our most cherished beliefs, concepts, ideas, opinions and prejudices. The conventional notion of time is a concept we cling to most obsessively, so it follows that this stands most in need of liberation.

The primary cause of our alienation from nature in general and our own higher natures in particular is the split time outlook that underlies the dualism of our western judeo-christian heritage. Sacred time has been transferred away from the natural world, thereby permitting the wanton destruction that is now taking place. There is not a strong enough built-in moral and spiritual motivation against such destructiveness. This is what we now need most urgently and this is why we also need to bring the idea of sustainable religion onto the green political agenda.

We will not save the world by dropping out and shunning politics. We will only save it by re-connecting higher values to the political process. This entails reuniting two 'worlds' previously seen as being radically separate: the hard world of power and political reality on the one hand and the soft world of wisdom, morality, spirituality on the other. To regard either or both worlds as irrelevant or irreconcilable is simply to perpetuate the status quo.

Our actions are the result of inner states of mind and ways of perceiving the world. Destruction of the environment can only be effectively prevented when it is stopped at its source: destructive attitudes and ways of thinking, repressive perceptions that prevent us from being more aware of our natural higher potential. If we want real change rather than minor superficial alterations, we need to allow these perceptual changes to take place at a deep level. In their own different ways, both Feuerbach and Krishnamurti help us to see more clearly in this deeper sense, while Merton provides an example of the spontaneous nature of this vision.

There are now countless alternative groups, sects and communities. While individually there is no shortage of strange and cranky New Age cults, viewed collectively the New Age represents a significant movement of inner energy away from dualism and analysis towards holism and synthesis. But much of the spiritual energy seems to be introverted, turned in on its own little world.

The ever-multiplying varieties of destructiveness that we now face are so vast and terrifying that we can no longer afford to go on thinking and acting in our old dissociated, mean and petty ways. Our ways of seeing need to match the scale of the many threats now confronting us.

We now need to restore higher values to the political process, so that the very thought of destroying the world becomes utterly inconceivable. Such destructiveness would then be seen as the ultimate act of sacrilege. Pantheistic societies see the world like this and the recovery of a similar vision in our society entails reclaiming values traditionally relegated to another world.

Only connect. . . When the two timeworlds are seen as one and therefore sacred, we shall witness the most inspiring social transformation imaginable. On rousing the dormant metaphysician in ourselves, we reactivate the visionary, the poet, the jester, the lover of life, the dancer, the singer. Our song is then in harmony with the natural rhythms of the world, of holy mother earth.

A LIVING PHILOSOPHY*

Just as we now urgently need a philosophy of peace in order to be able to respond more positively to the opportunities being presented in eastern Europe and the Soviet Union, so we also need to develop a more spiritual form of philosophy, in order to understand and integrate non-material phenomena.

Just as the cold warrior politicians are the very ones most lacking a positive philosophy of peace and are consequently the most hesitant and sceptical about the easing of tensions (they find it 'idealistic', 'naive' and 'unrealistic' to envisage a world without enemies), so those scientists and philosophers most addicted to reductionist materialism – which represents a 'cold war' against the human spirit – are the least prepared to understand non-material phenomena.

More and more people today, of all age groups, are turning away from materialism and seeking a spiritual or idealist view of life. Modern philosophy has for the most part long ago ceased trying to grapple with ultimate issues, on the grounds that it is fruitless to discuss abstract concepts lacking precise definition.

Many frustrated seekers turn to the east; others turn to the

---

* This chapter is mostly taken from an essay I wrote in the late sixties, published as a booklet entitled *A Living Philosophy* in 1973.

occult, astrology, spiritualism and so on. Often a good deal more heat than light is generated in this frantic flight from materialism. Countless systems, as old as the hills but dressed up in bright, new western attire, claim to meet all our spiritual needs and answer all our philosophical questions. But where in this metaphysical jungle do we find any truly rational basis for an idealist view of life?

In a desperate desire to seek instant new answers to timeless old questions, people turn here, there and everywhere. They overlook the possibility that there may already be a 'home-grown' western philosophy which, while not arrogantly and presumptuously claiming to answer all the questions, at least supplies a rational framework within which we can take a fresh look at problems that have long perplexed philosophers and scientists alike.

If certain non-material phenomena are a part of life, a part of nature, then it is only logical to suggest that we need a living philosophy in order to try and make some sense out of such phenomena. From a purely materialist standpoint, phenomena classified as 'spiritual,' 'psychic' or 'mystical' have no right to occur in the first place, so we are hardly likely to gain any understanding of such phenomena with a philosophy that does not even permit their occurrence. It is hardly surprising that psychic experiences are labelled 'para' normal and 'extra' sensory, yet to countless people they are a normal and natural part of life. To these people there is nothing 'extra' or 'para' about such phenomena.

William James stands out as one of the very few philosophers of modern times to have seriously explored psychic phenomena from an unbiased angle. But there is another philosopher who also took such phenomena seriously and whose name almost seems to have been forgotten: Henri Bergson.

Bergson drew a distinction between two different ways of perceiving reality. The first, which is predominantly cerebral-intellectual, is the familiar outside-in approach. It is linear, logical, analytical, objective. The second, which is predominantly intuitive-imaginative, is the inside-out approach. This form of perception does not rely on secondhand, culturally conditioned concepts and preconceptions. Instead it entails a process of intuitive empathy, or empathic intuition, whereby there is a close connection between observer and observed, subject and object.

Bergson greatly favoured the latter approach over the former, but the whole scientific ethos at the time was in the grip of a narrow, reductionist, anti-imaginative, ultra-analytical fashion that sometimes seemed very dogmatic, even fanatical, and from which science is only now beginning to emerge. Bergson's approach was a casualty of this passing fad and his name was anathema in the reductionist fortress. Now the world of quantum mechanics is revealing an aspect of reality very much closer to Bergson's vision. It is now no longer possible to draw such a clear and confident distinction between observer and observed, the whole and its parts.

The true purpose of knowledge or science is, according to Bergson, to really know things deeply, to touch the inner essence of things, to go far beyond mere superficial descriptions, labels, categories, to feel things from within – rather than standing aside, pretending not to be involved and trying to describe them from the outside:

> A true empiricism is that which proposes to get as near to the original itself as possible, to search deeply into its life, and so, by a kind of intellectual auscultation, to feel the throbbings of its soul: and this true empiricism is the true metaphysics.

The word 'auscultation' means listening with the aid of a stethoscope to the sounds coming from the organs inside the body, as a method of determining their health. Bergson uses this medical analogy in relation to our inner meta-physical health. Metaphysics thus defined involves 'in-feeling'; the German *Einfühlung* describes the process. There does not seem to be a satisfactory English equivalent; to feel deeply with, identify with, have compassion for that which we are trying to understand. This compassionate perception is a form of poetic empiricism or empirical poetry. The human face of science and the scientific face of art.

In order to be relevant to life in every sense of the word, philosophy itself must live and move. Static or dead metaphysical or theological systems might be compared to the advertisements one passes on the highway. Humanity moves on, leaving the advertisements behind. One or two ads may briefly catch one's eye, but one's attention soon returns to the business at hand: life. A dynamic, living philosophy moves with humanity, life and consciousness. It is not merely a billboard, framed and set apart from one. Instead, it accompanies one, since it is part of the phenomenon of life itself. We may not agree with every detail of any given philosophy, but without this inner living impetus, philosophy ceases to be relevant to life.

Henri Bergson is often thought of as belonging to the period 1890–1914,[1] but his philosophy is in fact of perennial relevance both to science and to religion. It is too dynamic to be restricted to a specific period and transcends passing fashions, fixed systems of thought and warring factions within philosophy. Whether or not a given philosophy is regarded at a given time as fashionable or unfashionable bears no necessary relation to its intrinsic value.

Life itself underlies all the debates and arguments, the misunderstandings and the divisions. The phenomenon of life bears witness to the fact that there must be a dimension where understanding and harmony can take place. Bergson went so far as to claim that it was possible *even for philosophers* to agree with each other on an intuitive level:

> Intuition, if it could be prolonged beyond a few instants, would not only make the philosopher agree with his own thought, but also all philosophers with each other. Such as it is, fugitive and incomplete, it is, in each system, what is

worth more than the system and survives it. The object of philosophy would be reached if this intuition could be sustained, generalized and, above all, assured of external points of reference in order not to go astray.[2]

Since Bergson's time modern philosophy has greatly improved its external points of reference. It is therefore in a better position to reappraise earlier philosophies that might temporarily have fallen by the wayside as innocent victims of the unphilosophical tendency to think in terms of fashion. Here we can only touch on a few of the salient features in the hope that others will continue this work, since the full implications of Bergson's philosophy have yet to be explored.

Henri Bergson was born in Paris in 1859 and died in Paris in 1941. His mother was English, his father Polish and from the latter, who was an accomplished musician, 'he doubtless inherited something of the artistic temperament which is reflected throughout his books.'[3] It is precisely because of his imaginative style of writing that Bergson holds little appeal for the analytical school of philosophy, or the disciples of Wittgenstein, Ryle or Ayer.

Bergson's first major work was published in 1889: his *Essai sur les données immédiates de la conscience,* translated in 1910 under the title of *Time and Free Will.* His second major work also came out in 1889: *Matière et Mémoire (Matter and Memory,* 1910). In 1900 Bergson was elected to the chair of modern philosophy at the Collège de France. His best known work, *l'Evolution créatrice,* was published in 1907 *(Creative Evolution,* 1911). The English edition of *An Introduction to Metaphysics* appeared in 1912 and his last major work, *The Two Sources of Morality and Religion,* in 1935. In 1913 Bergson was elected President of the Society for Psychical Research, an office held at various times by such distinguished men as Henry Sidgwick, F.W.H. Myers, William James, Gilbert Murray, William McDougall and, more recently, Professors C.D. Broad, H.H. Price and Sir Alister Hardy, F.R.S.

In *Time and Free Will* Bergson advances the idea of 'pure time' or 'real duration' *(durée réelle)*, as opposed to the artificial and mechanical concepts of time seen as a succession of discrete events. Pure time is wholly qualitative and cannot be measured. To claim that one can measure pure time merely by counting successive and separate events is an illusion: 'we give a mechanical explanation of a fact and then substitute the explanation for the fact itself.'[4] Proust was among those greatly influenced by Bergson's theories of time.

Bergson held that the great fallacy is to mix up space and time, viewing time in spatialized, static terms. Since time is dynamic, its true nature will obviously elude one if one can only think in static terms: we set our states of consciousness side by side in such a way as to perceive them simultaneously, no longer in one another, but alongside one another; in a word, we project time into space, we express duration in terms of extensity. Pure duration, on the other hand, is the form which the succession of our conscious states assumes when our ego lets itself *live,* when it refrains from separating its present state from its former states.

Eliminate superficial mental states and habitual ways of thinking and one can actually feel the qualitative, flowing nature of real duration, for example when dreaming. But Bergson held that even in the waking state, daily experience ought to teach us to distinguish between duration as quality (which is probably what animals perceive) and time materialized, time that has become quantity by being set out in space. The intuition of pure time has been thrust into the subconscious mind, largely for practical reasons:

> Consciousness, goaded by an insatiable desire to separate, substitutes the symbol for the reality, or perceives the reality only through a symbol. As the self thus refracted, and thereby broken to pieces, is much better adapted to the requirements of social life in general and language in

particular, consciousness prefers it and gradually loses sight of the fundamental self.[5]

Thus shadow and substance are confused and we are generally content with the shadow of the self projected into homogeneous space. It is consequently impossible to attain any self-knowledge without first altering one's habitual ways of thinking about time. One can feel, or at least imagine, the eternal flow of pure time, even if one cannot describe it, and via intuition and the imagination it is possible to view life under the form of eternity. A greater awareness of the eternal dimension underlying everyday existence completely alters one's whole outlook on life.

It would clearly be illogical to claim that the mere shadow or substitute of the true self is free. Freedom inevitably becomes an empty cliché if it only applies to the superficial self. The superficial self is largely an automaton, conditioned by habit and association. These reduce the self to an aggregate of conscious states, feelings and ideas: our daily actions are called forth not so much by our feelings themselves as by the unchanging images with which these feelings are bound up. In times of stress and crisis, however, our decisions can be genuinely free, for on these occasions the true self bursts through the artificial barriers normally imprisoning it: something may revolt. It is the deep-seated self rushing up to the surface. It is the outer crust bursting, suddenly giving way to an irresistible thrust.

It is perfectly reasonable and logical to believe in free will on the basis of one's intuitive experience of true freedom. In fact Bergson even stressed an element of certainty at this deeper level:

> The self, infallible when it affirms its immediate experiences, feels itself free and says so; but as soon as it tries to explain its freedom to itself it no longer perceives itself except *via* a kind of refraction through space. Hence a symbolism of a mechanical kind, equally incapable of proving, disproving or illustrating free will.[6]

The fact that freedom is intellectually indefinable in no way subtracts from its intuitive reality. If something is true within one's own experience, it is empirically valid. The level of consciousness at which a fact occurs or is experienced does not affect the validity of that fact. If science cannot yet fully account for intuitive facts, the fault lies with the present limitations of scientific method and the ideological presuppositions underlying it, rather than with the intuitive facts themselves, which form a natural part of human experience. When naturally occurring phenomena are relegated to the outer fringes of science, it is a sign that something is wrong with science.

In *Matter and Memory* Bergson is usually interpreted as being radically dualistic. The title of the work suggests some fundamental distinction between mind and matter. Even Bergson himself wrote in the preface that this book 'affirms the reality of spirit and the reality of matter and tries to determine the relation of the one to the other by the study of memory. It is, then, frankly dualistic. But . . . it deals with body and mind in such a way as, we hope, to lessen greatly, if not to overcome, the theoretical difficulties that have always beset dualism.' One wonders, however, whether Bergson's self-confessed dualism is not more apparent than real, for there are several passages in his writings where mind and matter seem to merge and ultimately Bergson would seem closer to a philosophy of idealist monism rather than dualism.

For a start, Bergson's definition of matter is not very materialistic; it is defined as 'an aggregate of "images" '. By 'image' is meant something more than the idealist's 'representation' or 'picture,' but something less than the realist's 'thing' or 'concrete object.' Memory is seen as the intersection or convergence of mind and matter. The body is seen as a centre of action that cannot give birth to a representation, a conductor or transformer standing between events affecting it and itself affecting other organs within the body.

Bergson's view of the brain deserves far more attention than it has received. He saw it as an organ of choice with a purely functional, practical role, certainly not a creative one: 'If images have survived, it is with a view to utility.'[7] The brain's main job is to censor mental images, only allowing through to consciousness those impressions, thoughts or ideas that are of practical, biological value.

In discussing Bergson's theory of the brain, Aldous Huxley coined the term 'cerebral reducing valve,'[8] which is a good way of putting it. The brain is seen by Bergson as a kind of telephone exchange; its role is to allow or to delay communication. The brain itself adds nothing to the messages received, but selects and sorts them; it might also be called a cerebral clearing house. Bergson rejected the naïve materialist tendency to equate mind and brain, on the logical and self-evident grounds that there is vastly more in a given occasion of consciousness than in the corresponding brain state.

It has been known for some time that removing part of the brain does not necessarily entail loss of a particular part of memory. Perplexed neurologists, brain specialists and psychologists would find that Bergson's theory of the brain, far from being obsolete, throws light on many contemporary problems and mysteries in this field. It seems most unlikely that such problems will ever be finally resolved on the basis of materialist theories of the brain.

Mental activity is so obviously more than the sum of its quantifiable cerebral parts that a holistic view seems the only logical position. In a later essay, Bergson wrote:

As the symphony overflows the movements which scan it,
so the mental life overflows the cerebral life. . . . The brain
is neither an organ of thought, nor of feeling, nor of
consciousness; but it keeps consciousness, feeling and
thought tensely strained on life, and consequently makes
them capable of efficacious action . . . the brain is the organ
of attention to life.[9]

The brain is the censor of the unconscious, where all the

past is remembered in pure memory, shutting out anything from the past that is not useful and relevant to the present. Cerebral activity responds to a very small part of mental activity, allowing through only a trickle of useful mental material. At a time when the brain is often worshipped as a cerebral god, it is salutary to consider this organ with a little more humility. It is undeniable that the brain is a natural masterpiece, an incredibly complex and wonderful organ, but it is a mistake to equate complexity with omniscience, least of all with originality and creativity. The values and feelings that mean most to us cannot be accounted for in terms of brain mechanics or brain chemistry.

There are ominous signs that a form of intellectual fascism is donning the mantle of social snobbery and other preju-dices. A high I.Q. does not make one person any better than another and to arrange society in the form of an intellectual pyramid, with brains at the top and non-brains at the bottom, is no more democratic than a feudal hierarchy with the king and nobles at the top and the mass of peasants at the bottom. It is dangerous to form intellectual élites and cliques con-vinced of their own cerebral superiority over lesser mortals.

The brain may well be better designed to promote forget-ting than remembering and it is clearly inadmissible to regard the brain as an elaborate filing system with all our memories physically stored in it. Something must prevent all the count-less images of pure memory from being simultaneously pre-sent to consciousness, which would make life extremely awk-ward from the practical point of view. The brain seems ideally designed to reduce awareness of biologically useless mental images. One can easily test this theory for oneself: the more one concentrates (i.e., the more one puts the brain to work) on a name or detail that one has temporarily forgot-ten, the less likely one is to recall it. The forgotten name or detail is more likely to come back in a moment of cerebral *relaxation* rather than cerebral tension.

Bergson believed that if one could disengage what one

observes now from the particular rhythm of duration that characterizes consciousness, one would know things in themselves, experienced from within as pure perception, not merely seen from without in a dissociated way. Blake expressed a similar view in his famous lines: 'If the doors of perception were cleansed, everything would appear to man as it is, infinite. For man has closed himself up, till he sees all things through narrow chinks of his cavern.'

Bergson held that a form of imaginative empathy, a placing of oneself mentally within the object, should be applied to the deepest and most intractable metaphysical problems: 'pure perception places us in matter and we penetrate spirit via pure memory.' While introspection may reveal a distinction between matter and spirit, 'it also bears witness to their union.' This is not as contradictory as it might appear, since the act of introspection itself involves both the brain, acting as censor, and extra-cerebral consciousness. The distinction between mind and matter tends to take place on the more superficial level of habitual intellectual reasoning, not on the deeper intuitive level, where all is one.

Bergson once speculated on what might have happened had modern science devoted all its energies to the study of the mental rather than the physical world:

> We should certainly have had a psychology of which today we can form no idea, any more than before Galileo we could have imagined what our physics would be: a psychology that probably would have been to our present psychology what our physics is to that of Aristotle. Foreign to every mechanistic idea . . . science would have enquired into, instead of dismissing *a priori,* facts; perhaps 'psychical research' would have stood out as its principal preoccupation.
>
> The most general laws of mental activity once discovered . . . we should have passed from mind to life: biology would have been constituted, but a vitalist biology, quite different from ours, which would have sought, behind the sensible forms of living beings, the inward invisible force of which

the sensible forms are the manifestations. On this force we have today taken no hold just because our science of mind is in its infancy; and this is why men of science are not wrong when they reproach vitalism with being a sterile doctrine: it is sterile today, it will perhaps not be so always, and it probably would not have been so now had modern science at its origin taken things at the other end.

Together with this vitalist biology there would have arisen a medical practice which would have sought to remedy *directly* the insufficiencies of the vital force: it would have aimed at the cause and not at the effects, at the centre instead of at the periphery; healing by suggestion might have taken forms and proportions of which it is impossible for us to form the least idea.[10]

Bergson's evolutionary vitalism is the dominant theme of *Creative Evolution,* which could be described as a metaphysical *Origin of Species.* Appropriately enough, Bergson was in fact born in the same year that *The Origin of Species* was published and his philosophy adds a missing dimension to Darwinian theory, which, as it stands, is incomplete and thus apt to be misleading.

The biologist, Sir Alister Hardy, advocated a reappraisal of Darwinian theory in his Gifford Lectures for 1964–65, published as *The Living Stream* and *The Divine Flame.* The subtitle of the first volume reads, 'A Restatement of Evolution Theory and its Relation to the Spirit of Man,' and in this volume Hardy advances the tentative hypothesis of a psychic pool or blueprint, somewhat analogous to the Jungian collective unconscious, linking living creatures with a form and behaviour pattern outside time, parallel to the DNA process.[11] Hardy even suggests in the second volume that the living stream of evolution may be as much divine as physical in nature.[12]

Ever since Descartes it has been taken for granted in the west that consciousness is confined exclusively to human beings, while animals are mere automata. Even the churches have given this facet of cartesian thought their official blessing in denying souls to animals, thus paving the way for abuses such as vivisection and factory farming.

But Bergson insisted that consciousness was not even confined to organisms with brains: 'It would be as absurd to refuse consciousness to an animal because it has no brain as to declare it incapable of nourishing itself because it has no stomach.'[13] An eminent neurologist, Lord Brain, has voiced a similar opinion: 'In evolution it is very difficult to find any point in the scale of life at which mind cannot be said to exist . . . and I know of no reason for denying consciousness in some elementary form to comparatively simple organisms. If this is so, at what point in the scale of evolution does mind make its appearance?'[14]

Brain also believes that the unconscious mind, in the Jungian sense, may play a vitalizing role in art and religion and that science also owes a debt to the unconscious, which supplies hunches and intuitions which are not the results of conscious rational thought but which are nevertheless important for scientific progress. Brain asks: 'When we have reduced everything to the ultimate units of matter, whatever they may currently be, have we really done anything more than is involved in explaining a cathedral by saying that it is built of bricks?'

Just as Russia underwent destalinization, so science must now undergo a dematerialization of its basic doctrines. Darwinian theory left us with a mechanistic, deterministic picture of humankind and nature; the Copernican revolution gave us a clockwork image of the universe – predictable, cold and lifeless. Modern advances in astronomy, however, reveal that space is not so empty or so lifeless after all and is in fact far more biological in character.

Bergson further expounds his philosophy of rational mysticism in *An Introduction to Metaphysics,* which has been described as 'a philosophical interpretation of biology which culminates in a sweeping metaphysical vision not unlike that of Plotinus.'[15] Pure intuition and the essential identity of the individual soul in man with the universal world-soul were ideas central to Neoplatonist philosophy. Plotinus saw nature as a contemplative and creative energy, also foreshadowing Bergson's life force (*élan vital*). Like Bergson, Plotinus believed that the primary task of philosophy is to attain direct intuitive knowledge, a form of mystical union beyond words and symbols.

Bergson saw metaphysics as the science which claims to dispense with symbols. There is one reality which must be seized from within by intuition, not viewed analytically from without. Intuition is the metaphysical investigation of that which is essential and unique in any phenomenon. Far too much philosophy, and for that matter theology, skirts round its subject matter as though afraid to get too close to the truth. Bergson believed that metaphysics should penetrate to the very heart of knowledge as integral experience. It must therefore go beyond all shadows and immerse itself in the underlying substance. The true nature of any given phenomenon or process is far more than the sum of the words used to describe them.

The life force constitutes the unique nature of all that is animate. It is the fundamental cause of the variations which produce new species and, as the ultimate principle of existence, it is the creative power that rolls through all things. The intellect alone, unaided by intuition, cannot possibly form an adequate idea of the life force: 'Seeking the original in the translation where naturally it cannot be, it denies the existence of the original on the grounds that it is not found in the translation.' The intellect without intuition seems ideally designed to create such vicious circles. Habitual ways of thinking about metaphysical problems condemn philosophy to an eternal skirmishing between schools and installs contradiction in the very heart of the object and of the method. The only way out of this dilemma consists in placing oneself within the object itself by an effort of intuition. Rather than going from concepts to the object of knowledge, one should first experience knowledge intuitively and only then resort to the use of concepts: 'To philosophize, therefore, is to invert the habitual direction of the work of thought.'

Bergson saw matter as a devitalized form of life which moves in a direction opposite to vitalized life. He also wrote: 'Matter is necessity, consciousness is freedom. This is what life is: freedom inserting itself within necessity, turning it to its own use.'[16] Matter could also be compared to a star: it is always unmaking itself, expending its energy, whereas consciousness is unceasingly creating new life forms. In evolution it is as if an immense current of consciousness had traversed matter, drawing it towards organization and turning it into an instrument of freedom. No artificial form of so-called 'life' could ever be endowed with the vital impetus which gives life its own creative power and uniqueness.

There is no reason why intuition should conflict with science: 'How could there be any disharmony between our intuitions and our science if these intuitions are something like instinct – an instinct conscious, refined, spiritualized – and if instinct is still nearer life than intellect and science?' asked Bergson. Intuition is the missing link between science and metaphysics: 'a truly intuitive philosophy would realize the much desired union of science and metaphysics.'

Bergson did not believe that it was possible to attain truth by studying the mechanism of thinking, criticizing the critical faculties and analyzing language. He recommended a much more direct approach:

I see only one means of knowing how far I can go, that is by going. If the knowledge one seeks is real, then to analyze the mechanism of thought before seeking knowledge could only show the impossibility of ever getting it, since we should be studying thought before the expansion of it which it is the business of knowledge to obtain.[17]

There is an attractive Gallic *panache* and practical directness about this approach to metaphysics, bringing alive an other-

wise moribund subject. Academic philosophers and theologians have managed to keep metaphysics and mysticism
respectively beyond the reach of ordinary people, but the
time has now come for us to claim our own birthright. We
should take pride in the fact that we are amateur philosophers, since this means literally that we love the truth twice
over. Bergson saw no reason why one should not try and
explore levels of consciousness beyond time and space:

> If there be a beyond for conscious beings, I cannot see why
> we should not be able to discover the means to explore it.
> Nothing which concerns man is likely to conceal itself
> deliberately from the eyes of man. Sometimes, moreover,
> the information we imagine to be far off, even infinitely
> distant, is at our side, waiting only till it pleases us to notice
> it.[18]

There is a passage in *The Varieties of Religious Experience*
where William James expresses a strikingly similar view:

> Our normal waking consciousness, rational consciousness as
> we call it, is but one special type of consciousness, whilst
> all about it, parted from it by the filmiest of screens, there
> lie potential forms of consciousness entirely different. We
> may go through life without suspecting their existence; but
> apply the requisite stimulus, and at a touch they are there
> in all their completeness, definite types of mentality which
> probably somewhere have their fields of application and
> adaptation. No account of the universe in its totality can be
> final which leaves these other forms of consciousness quite
> disregarded.[19]

If materialist theory is correct in claiming that the brain
corresponds to the totality of human consciousness, then
obviously physical death would entail a complete and final
end. 'But,' claimed Bergson, 'if the mental life overflows the
cerebral life, if the brain only translates into movements a
small part of what occurs in consciousness, then survival
becomes so probable that the onus of proof falls on him who
denies it rather than on him who affirms it.'

The essence of Bergson's philosophy is that in order to understand the movement of life one must move with life rather than viewing it from a detached and static position. It is a philosophy of change.

Philosophy has wrestled with this problem of change or flux for many centuries. The pre-socratics Anaximander and Heraclitus both subscribed to philosophies of change. Anaximander believed in eternal motion and evolution. His belief that humans were descended from fishes was a remarkable prevision of Darwinian theory, considering he lived more than two thousand years before Darwin. He also believed in a dynamic form of cosmic or divine justice similar to karma. Like Bergson, Heraclitus believed that everything is becoming: 'You cannot step twice into the same river since fresh waters are forever flowing in upon you.'

There was always a radical distinction in Greek thought between the mystical and the dialectic. This distinction still profoundly affects western thought, but it was never present in Hinduism, which has always succeeded in being both a philosophy and a religion. Bergson's philosophy makes possible a similar reunion in western thought. One has first to move with life before one can understand any permanent, changeless ultimate truths underlying life, beyond movement. The search for permanence, at any rate in western philosophy, seems to have begun with Parmenides, who believed in the oneness of all things and the indestructibility of what later came to be called substance. In this respect Parmenides seems to foreshadow Spinoza.

The problem of flux and permanence is not a purely academic matter of no relevance to daily life. There is sometimes a painful conflict between the generations, the older generation tending to be conservative and settled, the younger generation tending to be radical and restless. It is usually assumed that the two mentalities are irreconcilable, certainly when it comes to politics. But it is in fact perfectly possible to combine a political philosophy of continuous non-violent change with a substantially permanent and changeless form of metaphysics. Gandhi is a notable example.

Systems of every sort – philosophical, religious and political – must be subject to change, but without some idea of permanence underlying all the systems and ideologies, it is easy to get caught up in a deadly boring, selfish and potentially dangerous treadmill of permanent revolution for its own sake as an end in itself.

The social, ethical and religious implications of the life force are discussed in Bergson's last work, *The Two Sources of Morality and Religion*. As with time, memory and perception, Bergson also divides morality, religion and society each into two main types: traditional morality and ideal morality, static and dynamic religion, the open and the closed society.

It is impossible, according to Bergson, to explain the origins of ideal morality as mere modifications of traditional morality. The latter speaks for an existing order which demands to be preserved and perpetuated, whereas ideal morality speaks for a vision which inspires in sensitive people a demand that the existing order be radically changed. Those mystical elements in the teachings of religious prophets that are not subject to the vicissitudes of history and tradition act as magnets to the rest of humanity, drawing us upwards.

Exceptional people, moral leaders, mystics and saints are those who have placed themselves consciously in the current of the life force: 'All great mystics declare that they have the impression of a current passing from their soul to God and flowing back again from God to mankind.'[20] Reason alone does not constitute human dignity: there are, behind reason, the people who have made humankind divine. It is they who draw us towards an ideal society, while we yield to the pressure of the real one.

Analogous to traditional morality is static religion and opposed to this is the dynamic religion which has its source in mysticism:

True mystics simply open their souls to the oncoming wave. Sure of themselves, because they feel within them something better than themselves, they prove to be great men of action, to the surprise of those to whom mysticism is nothing but visions and raptures and ecstasies. That which they have allowed to flow into them is a stream flowing down and seeking through them to reach their fellow-men; the necessity to spread around them what they have received affects them like an onslaught of love.[21]

There is probably a mystic in each one of us: 'If a word of a great mystic finds an echo in one or another of us, may it not be that there is a mystic dormant within us, merely waiting for an occasion to awake?' Bergson defines mysticism as the establishment of contact with the creative effort life itself manifests: 'This effort is of God, if it is not God himself.' Mysticism involves a superabundance of life and joy, a boundless impetus resulting from direct apprehension of the divine.

The mysticism of dynamic religion is a means of bringing about humanity's great ethical leap forward beyond the limits of the closed society with its egocentric outlook, into the outward-looking open society. The spread of genuine mysticism must ultimately create an open society whose freedom and spontaneity will express the life force which pervades the universe. Bergson believed that democracy was in principle capable of providing social and political frameworks conducive to an open society. But in practice the modern so-called democratic nation-states tend to be closed, inward-looking societies based on national self-interest rather than international altruism.

In view of the breakdown of traditional, static religion, Bergson believed that spirituality held out some promise by restoring to people the belief that life is more than one long grind of work, worry, money and escapist pastimes. Once traditional religion itself degenerates into another form of escapism, it obviously loses the capacity to raise our sights to higher goals and simply descends to the level of other trivial escapist pastimes. Spirituality carries on where static religion has failed.

If philosophy has tended increasingly to be a subject for academic experts only, true mysticism has hitherto been reserved for an even smaller minority of exceptional men and women. Bergson shows that both philosophy and mysticism are within the reach of the ordinary man and woman, drawing them upwards to a higher and more joyful plane of existence. The time has now come to question the traditional approach to mysticism and ask if the direct apprehension of the divine is not intended for all of us here on earth, as part of our natural evolutionary birthright. This may indeed be the only alternative to chaos and annihilation.

In the present age we must surely have reached saturation point in materialism, in all spheres of life: in science, in politics, in economics, in philosophy, even in religion. Either we are going to allow materialism to destroy us, or we are going to penetrate beyond the god Matter to a new age where mind, the spirit, creativity and genuine idealism predominate. Bergson's philosophy provides a foundation on which this idea, hitherto a dream, could be turned into reality.

APPENDIX

We have barely begun to think globally in the deeper sense. Global thinking has hitherto been largely exploitative, exemplified by vast multinational corporations, the World Bank and the worldwide arms trade. To counter these destructive forms of global thinking, we need an ecologically benign overview of the world. This obviously cannot be based on purely materialist premises, which at present underpin the more harmful forms of global thinking. As I have argued throughout this book, we need a 'reinvestment in sacred values'.

The following piece is reprinted from the Gandhian review, *The Acorn,* because it brings together many strands at a more philosophical level, providing a basis for more enlightened political action. Stephen Nachmanovitch is a composer, writer and computer artist. Abdul Aziz Said is Professor at the School of International Service, The American University, Washington DC and has been an active participant in Arab-Israeli peace dialogues.

GLOBAL THINKING*

A Call for Reinvestment in Sacred Values

by Stephen Nachmanovitch and Abdul Aziz Said

We live in a time when we risk making our world uninhabit-able. In times of danger, it is normal for us to look to some outside threat, to look for 'causes'. But in the situation we face today, we must look inward as well as outward. We are coming to realize that our whole approach to Earth's prob-lems needs to be altered: even the best-informed and best-intentioned attempts to improve things often end up making them worse. The worldwide ecological crisis, of which the nuclear weapons threat is only the most obvious of many interrelated facets, is fundamentally a crisis of mind and spirit.

Our technological abilities are advancing exponentially with time. Our moral and spiritual abilities are not. In the course of evolution human beings have become the custod-ians of life on earth; but we threaten the very existence of life unless we can correct our own lopsided development. We might wish that we could press a magical button that would eliminate all weapons of mass destruction from this planet. But if we cannot change our own deeply ingrained habits of thinking, feeling, sensing, and acting that gave birth to those weapons in the first place, the weapons would be recreated in short order. By habit we think of national secur-ity in terms of military forces and capabilities. By habit we think that one people's interests can only be served at the expense of another. Such habits of thought become deeply embedded in our every day life as what we call 'common sense'. Our whole way of thinking and seeing such matters needs to be renovated from the inside out.

* First printed in *The Acorn – A Gandhian Review*, March 1987, II, 1, pp. 13–16 and reproduced here by kind permission of the editor.

We ask here: What are the hidden, addictive patterns that we must confront?

Every person, every culture, operates a (usually unconscious) *epistemology,* which predisposes us to emphasize certain kinds of perception, learning, and action, and predisposes us to ignore others. Each of us is hypnotized from infancy on into perceiving the world in accordance with suggestions we have absorbed from the surrounding culture. At the core of any culture are tacit understandings about the nature of human aspirations, relationships to one another and to the universe, the source of ultimate authority, which are largely unspoken, untaught, and unquestioningly assumed. In industrial society these include something like the following:

– Ultimate authority resides in the testimony of the physical senses and the reasoning analytical mind.
– What is real (or at least what is important) is what is measurable.
– Knowledge is primarily an instrument of power and domination over unpredictable and sinister forces of nature, and, ultimately, over social forces as well.
– As individual persons we are separate and autonomous, predominantly seeking goals that relate to our physical well-being and self-gratification.

These elements of our epistemology, as well as other related, tacit understandings:

(a) have been responsible for the great gains in material standard of living and the technological achievements of Western industrial society;
(b) are now at the very root of the global dilemmas that have recently become apparent;
(c) are now, because our survival is at stake, in the process of change.

Epistemology is usually defined as the theory of knowledge: it deals with questions like: how do we know? what do we know? how do we sort our perceptual input into categories like 'knowledge', 'opinion', 'trivia', 'nonsense', 'hallucination', etc.? In the 1940s Gregory Bateson and Warren McCulloch transplanted this word into biology, because they realized that even a rat in a learning experiment 'has' an epistemology, an internalized theory of knowledge that calibrates its perceptual biases. Epistemology thus becomes greatly extended in meaning to include, for example, the neural filtering that sensitizes a frog's eye to small moving dots that are likely to be flies – or the cultural filtering that sensitizes a person to believe or disbelieve in miracles, or in economic determinism.

We typically underestimate the power of belief and knowledge. Ideas such as 'Christian love,' 'holy war,' 'the Aryan master race,' 'manifest destiny,' 'the chosen people,' 'the white man's burden,' have shaped history. Belief in a now outmoded theory of evolution that stressed 'struggle for existence' and 'survival of the fittest' gave economic and political thinking in this century the moral imperatives of 'social Darwinism.' The use of physical science to generate new technologies has fundamentally impacted on our lives in ways so numerous and familiar as to scarcely require mention.

People from cultures that embody differing epistemologies will see reality differently. 'The Sun's light when He unfolds it,' wrote Blake, 'Depends on the organ that beholds it' (*Auguries of Innocence*). Epistemology is the sieve through which we pass reality to decide[1] which realities are more real than the others.

Epistemology in action: A psychologist in the 1940s using a tachistoscope (a projector that flashes images on a screen for only a tiny fraction of a second) shows American city dwellers a subway scene in which a well-dressed black man is attacked by a shabbily-dressed white man. The subjects report seeing a well-dressed white man being attacked by a shabbily-dressed black man.

Epistemology in action: A President of the United States is told by his advisors that to base his foreign policy on human rights considerations is 'unrealistic.'

The strength inherent in our rational, materialistic epistemology is the speed and efficiency with which we are able to master special-purpose technologies. The weakness inherent in that same epistemology is that we tend to ignore context and the long-term consequences of our acts. We create magnificent amenities to improve our lives and are then surprised to discover the harmful 'side-effects': pollution, exhaustion of resources, starvation, and war.

In New York City in 1906 the horses were daily depositing 60,000 gallons of urine and 2,000,000 pounds of manure on the city streets. The invention brought in to clean up this pollution was: the internal combustion engine!

Jacques Prevert wrote: 'The road to Hell is paved with good inventions.'

Governments characteristically try to buy national security with weaponry: they arm themselves and cement 'friend-ships' by arming other governments. The cause of armament (we leave out the profit motive for the time being!) is a desire for security. The effect of armament is greater insecurity, which leads to more and more armament.

This vicious circle of runaway feedback is the classical pattern of addiction. The addict is hungry for some intangible, like love or contentment; somehow a material thing like heroin or chocolate bars or money has become falsely identified in the addict's unconscious epistemology as a substitute. So he consumes more and more substances whilst his real needs are progressively less and less satisfied.

Love, safety, contentment, and national security are contexts. Heroin, chocolate bars, money, and MX missiles are things. Contexts and things are two different levels of reality.

One level cannot substitute for another: this is the basic rule of epistemology established by Korzybski when he said 'The map is not the territory.' Bateson applied this rule to psychiatry and to the psychological roots of the ecological crisis when he showed that madness, in one form or another, is the likely result when we try to substitute one level of reality for another.

The thought-forms we predominantly use in academia, in governments and courts of law, in the press, in social planning, are modeled on Aristotelian logic. What we need instead are thought-forms that are structured in the same way that our world is structured.

And what sort of structure is that? Take a look at one of those charts of the body's metabolic pathways that are always tacked up on the walls of biochemistry labs. What we see is an immensely complex network of loops which represent interconnected, interdependent chemical reactions whose products all feed back upon each other – a homeostatic circuit. There are no straight lines in such a chart, and to think in terms of 'causes' and 'effects' makes sense only if we cut out a portion of a circuit and treat it as though it were a whole entity.

We complicate problems of international relations due to our inability to perceive context and long-range consequences. Our information is always incomplete; natural, biological systems are always more complex and circuitous than our ideas about them.[2] Using lineal, cause–and–effect thinking to map a world that is an interconnected, interdependent network of feedback circuits inevitably leads to inappropriate actions that return to plague the inventors. Such thinking leads us to falsely regard the world as an object that can be manipulated rather than a home that must be lived in and with.

It is conventional now to think that ecological values are somehow in conflict with economic values, and that we are faced with an either/or choice between taking care of our environment vs. taking care of ourselves. But this is nonsense. The words 'ecology' and 'economy' are identical: they mean 'study of the house' in Greek. They refer to housekeeping. The physiology of the human body, the complexities of family life, the network of global trade, and the infinitely varied and delicate interdependencies of the totality of life on earth, are alike in structure. There exists in Buddhist mythology something called 'Indra's net': an immense, multiply-interconnected latticework of jewels each of which reflects all the others at once – what we now call a hologram. This is a very accurate description of how our world really is.

In Darwin's theory of evolution, the unit that evolves is the organism or species. In Bateson's theory of evolution, the unit that evolves is organism-plus-environment. The horse does not evolve, the grass does not evolve; rather the system horse-plus-grass co-evolves.

We try to maximize U.S. 'interests' and then wonder why our policies backfire or produce the opposite of the intended effects. The reason is that we are thinking in terms of an incorrect unit of analysis. A correct unit is nation-plus-environment, interest-group-plus-environment.

The equivalent (epistemologically false) unit of analysis at the level of daily life is the individual 'me' or 'ego'.

Perhaps the main factor that gave rise to the dilemmas of modern civilization was the myth of body/mind dualism, matter/spirit dualism, and the associated concept of the person as an individual surrounded by skin, with a distinct inside and outside. In other civilizations, 'progress' had been associated more with the perfection of the human soul within the wholeness of society and the universe. Early Christianity saw the individual as being born for immortality, born to go beyond himself, for, as St. Augustine stated, to be human is to be more than merely human. This also implies that to seek to be merely human, to maximize narrowly concerned human interests, is to fall below the human to the subhuman level, as the history of the modern world amply demonstrates.

Viable units of evolution are always expressed in terms that involve wholeness, context, community. Self – other, me – environment, yield the big-self or true-self of Jungian psychology or of the various mystical traditions in Vedantism, Kabbalah, Christianity, Buddhism, and Sufism. Schools of mystical training or self-development the world over invariably involve a process of dissolving excessive identification with the little-self.

The world community is now threatened by the very mechanisms which, in the past, have served an evolutionary purpose, and, because humans did not until recently possess the technology to render their environment lethal, were at least evolutionarily tolerable. But now we have run out of room. The competitive mechanisms that are still taught as the subject matter of international relations cannot serve us well in a finite, spherical, homeostatically interconnected world. We have moved into a new context for humanity as a whole. We need to be committed to a world which includes everyone. This idea is alien or at best seems like a pipe dream to present-day national leaders who continue to look at the world in terms of a competitive epistemology. Whether this idea is regarded as 'impossible' or not is itself a matter of epistemology. We know it is possible in practice because that is the way Earth's biosphere has been functioning for some hundreds of millions of years.

Since rational, materialistic epistemology came to define the direction of Western culture in post-Renaissance times (with roots going far back into antiquity), we have progressively denied the reality of those processes that relate (re-ligio) us to context and environment: namely art, dreams, religion, and other roads to the unconscious. Meanwhile, the conquest of the New World, Africa and Asia was bringing great wealth into Europe and creating a new mercantile society which saw in its power to manipulate the world the possibility of perfecting it in a material and economic sense. Parallel with this development, the role of the messiah in rejuvenating the Kingdom of God on Earth became converted into that of the revolutionary bringing about the perfect social order through revolutionary and violent means. Marxism, for example, is a Western religion based on the idea of inevitable material progress and merging messianic ideas with utopianism. However, such attempts at social change usually backfire, due to the inevitable narrowness of outlook. As Blake wrote during the Napoleonic Wars:

> *The hand of Vengeance found the Bed*
> *To which the purple Tyrant fled;*
> *The iron hand crushed the tyrant's head*
> *And became a tyrant in his stead.*

THE PICKERING MANUSCRIPT

Both Marxism and Capitalism (which are two sides of the same coin) tend to become exclusively preoccupied with material well-being, committing the epistemological error of mistaking the part for the whole. Both spiritual and esthetic matters are dismissed in these systems as archaic or disreputable or irrelevant.

However, just as we find that the naive materialism of the post-Renaissance centuries is not working out in the long run, things have begun to change in the direction of a more inclusive epistemology. With the rediscovery of depth psychology at the turn of the century (thanks to Dostoyevsky, Freud, Jung, and others) we have come to recognize the reality of the unconscious. We have begun to recover some of the material that was lost from industrial culture. Now, towards the end of the twentieth century, we are discovering[3] that the deeper we delve into the fundamentals of science, the closer they approach the fundamentals of many of the traditional mythologies and mysticisms. We are now coming to recognize the reality of the sacred.

Concurrently, biologists, historians and other scholars are developing an increasingly substantial foundation for the 'Gaia hypothesis,' which recognizes that the Earth itself is in fact a single living organism.

Perhaps no finding in the social and psychological sciences is so well established as the discovery (more accurately, rediscovery) that the greater portion of our mental activity goes on outside of conscious awareness. We believe, choose, and know unconsciously as well as consciously. Yet we typically live, think, and behave without taking seriously the implications of that finding. Our lives are probably more affected by the beliefs we hold unconsciously than by our conscious beliefs. The conscious beliefs (e.g. that the earth travels around the sun) may be changed by rather straightforward educational processes. More deeply held, partially conscious beliefs (e.g. that I am basically inadequate or unworthy) are not so easily changed, and their re-examination in psychotherapy often entails considerable inner struggle. Still more deeply held unconscious premises (e.g. about the basic nature of myself and my relationship to the universe) may be formed early in life and remain essentially unchanged throughout life; if they are altered it is likely to be in the context of a life trauma of major proportion.

We believe unconsciously; therefore we choose unconsciously. The unconscious choices are often in conflict with the conscious ones. The Freudian superego, an authoritarian inner parent, chooses certain behaviors and goals and punishes deviations with guilt feelings. Another part of the self, some sort of deep intuition, knows the directions of wholesome growth and development and gently guides these directions. Unless the various fragments of the self can be induced to align their choosing in the same direction, inner conflict is unavoidable. The person in whom an integration of the inner fragments is more or less accomplished we recognize as a person of integrity.

Research in biofeedback training discloses that we know unconsciously how to relax muscle tensions, change brain waves, alter heartbeat or blood pressure, change flow of blood and skin temperature – but we don't know we know without the feedback signal to instruct us.

We now find ourselves, as individuals, as nation-states, and as a species, involved in a period of intense and often bewildering transformation. The systems of government, production, culture, thought, perception, to which we have become accustomed and which have functioned for so long, are not working. This presents us with a challenge: shall we cling to that which is passing, or has already passed, or can we remain accessible to, can we even surrender to, the creative process without insisting that we know in advance the ultimate outcome for us, our institutions, our planet? To accept this challenge is to cherish freedom, to embrace life, and to find meaning.

Freedom of the individual is not the ability to manipulate life. It is the ability to experience life as it is. The experience of existence is a reflection of Being which is beauty and consciousness. Freedom is that which makes this experience accessible to the individual.

In this discussion, 'the sacred' is defined as any process that explicitly links us back to the largest possible context to which we belong.

Among the Sufis, who represent the mystical dimension of Islam, the most important daily practice or litany is called the *zikr*, which means 'remembrance.' This is not a bad name for the issue that here confronts us: remembering where we come from; remembering what we are; remembering what we are part of. Unity is never absent from us, but seldom realized.

The role of the prophet (in all of us) is then not the

simpleminded notion of someone who can foretell the future, but rather someone who reminds us of what has always been there, bringing rejuvenation to the world around.

The *zikr* invokes a state of mind called *tawhid,* which means unity of existence, the direct personal experience of Reality, the grasping of our relation to the absolute, and maintenance of harmony with the universe. Invoking this unity does not deny the apparent existence of a multiplicity of created things. Multiplicity is due to single reality being filtered through differing points of view rather than to the intrinsic nature of things. The world is more than a collection of persons and things.

The same phenomenon appears in the Buddhist tradition. This is why in the Zen sutras it says that there is no attainment, and nothing to be attained. They make a declaration, a personal stand, in the Four Great Vows of Buddhism:

> *Sentient beings are numberless: I vow to save them.*
> *Delusions are inexhaustible: I vow to put an end to them.*
> *The Dharmas are boundless: I vow to master them.*
> *The Buddha way is unsurpassable: I vow to attain it.*

(Dharma, like tawhid, refers us to the overall harmony and patterning of the universe, to Natural Law in the broadest possible sense, or to the place and fittingness and obligation of each individual human being in support of that pattern. Gregory Bateson, when once asked to define 'sacrament,' said 'Recognition of the pattern which connects.' 'Buddha,' which translates literally as 'the one who woke up,' refers not just to a historical personage but to any human being in the state of mind of full awareness which means a person is dedicated to the support of the total patterning and harmony of our world.)

Divine will functions in all phases of human history and in all aspects of human life. It is not relegated to the beginnings of creation as in eighteenth- and nineteenth-century

Deism, but is eternally present and eternally integrated with human responsibility.

Our current research into the fundamentals of science shows increasingly the common ground on which science, religion, art and philosophy stand. Our current discoveries of the tenuous nature of Earth's ecology and human stewardship of this world show the vital necessity of recognizing and re-orienting ourselves to that common ground, reinvesting the sacred into our daily activity and reinvesting ourselves in the sacred.

Scientists of an earlier generation were guilty of over-claiming when they dismissed religion as pre-scientific theorizing about matters on which scientists would eventually have a later word, if not the last. To be sure, the religionists were myopic and vulnerable to criticism when they insisted that characteristics of the physical world – such as the relative positions of the earth and sun – should be established by holy writ rather than empirical observation. But the scientists, on the other hand, were equally narrow-minded in insisting that all the religious traditions of the world were based in illusion since the realm of human experience they took as central was not empirically verifiable.

We need to cultivate a vision for the development of our identity as a planetary species that is whole and cooperative. Cooperative global development means a multiplication of all possible dimensions of human life. A developed country is one where obstacles to human freedom, community, and creativity have been eliminated, or better yet, absorbed and transcended.

Individual and societal growth are one and the same; each person is part of this open-ended process. Development is conscious, participatory, self-managed, cooperative, and seeks the full humanization of the person. Culture is a resource. Culture can be a unifying force for cooperative global politics. Creation, in the arts, science, technology, and daily life, is essentially a communal process, a primary source of human realization. Creativity can replace conformity as the primary mode of political action. We need a profoundly healing vision of cooperative global politics. The distinction between First, Second, and Third Worlds is a dangerous illusion; there is only one interdependent world, and this is it. Oppressor and oppressed are united in their mutually addictive pattern, whether they know it or not. This is the only planet we have.

The material and spiritual worlds are one. We need to redefine freedom away from a purely individualistic doing of one's own thing, both for people and societies. The individual can no longer be seen as the victim of society. The goal of freedom, and of development, is human creativity, the enhancement and elaboration of life. Creativity always involves a certain amount of discipline, self-restraint, and self-sacrifice. Planning and spontaneity become one. Reason and intuition become two faces of truth. Propositional knowledge and anecdotal knowledge become the two faces of storytelling.

We envision a cooperative global economics based on love, sacrifice, and cooperation, supporting individual and communal self-reliance, fair distribution of the earth's resources, caring for the planet, and control of human destructiveness. In such a world global and personal concerns inevitably fuse.

Reinvestment of the sacred means the humanizing of the sacred: the destruction of idols, which are delusive belief systems. It also refers to the consecration of the human, the recognition that sacred activity is not separate from immediate, personal, interpersonal experience. Our being together on this planet becomes, then, a sacred day-to-day reality, and what we call God becomes human. This seemingly impossible process of transformation has already begun, though it is often hard to see the signs. The signs are waiting to be created by us, here, today.

POSTSCRIPT

As this book goes to press, the Pentagon describes its priorities for the 1990s as 'robust nuclear posture and strategic defence, technological superiority, versatile, ready, deployable force and continued maritime superiority' (*The Guardian*, 30 January 1990). In its determination to sustain 'a strong forward-deployed military presence overseas', the US Defence Department plans to build up not only its strategic nuclear weapons systems but also mobile ICBM systems, the B-2 Stealth bomber, an additional Trident submarine, 52 Trident II missiles and an increased $4.5 billion for Star Wars. As far as British procurement is concerned, a defence expert has stated that no significant changes can take place within the next five to fifteen years, 'because everything is locked in concrete and the juggernaut keeps rolling on'.

In grudgingly accepting the decision to run down 3 out of some 90 US bases and installations in Britain, the Foreign Secretary referred to talks with his American counterpart in terms of 'how to build upon the Alliance's success after winning the cold war'. Mr Hurd did not explain how the continuing threat of nuclear omnicide can be 'won'. Psychologically, the cold war certainly does not seem to be over yet as far as the west is concerned.

In electing as their President a writer of such moral courage as Vaclav Havel, the people of Czechoslovakia have leapt in one bound from repression to a new, post-cold war cultural reawakening. Meanwhile we are still ruled by politicians who are prepared to press the button and whose thinking remains set in cold war concrete. Our western versions of the Securitate and Stasi remain firmly in place, still unaccountable to the public and still continuing to perpetrate their dirty tricks. At the cultural, moral and spiritual levels, we have not yet enjoyed our version of the Prague Spring of '68. But now the winds of change are blowing from east to west and more and more people in the west are beginning to notice that they too have been living in a state of moral and spiritual repression all these years.

NOTES

I Inner-Outer Connections

1. Somerville is the founder of International Philosophers for the Prevention of Nuclear Omnicide.
2. D. Hill, *The Independent*, 17 June 1988.
3. G.J. Whitrow, *The Nature of Time* (London; Penguin Books, 1975), p. 17.
4. L. Mumford, *Technics and Civilization* (London; Routledge & Kegan Paul, 1934).
5. M.J. Shallis, *The Silicon Idol* (Oxford; Oxford University Press, 1984), p. 139.
6. B. Wood, *Alias Papa – A Life of Fritz Schumacher* (London; Jonathan Cape, 1984), p. 363.
7. D. Hay, *Exploring Inner Space* (London; Penguin Books, 1982), p. 212.
8. *Seville Statement on Violence* (16 May 1986), quoted in *Psychologists for Peace Newsletter* (Winter, 1986) pp. 9 and 10.
9. M. Midgley, *Evolution as a Religion* (London: Methuen Books, 1985), p. 1.
10. J. Taylor, *The Scripture Doctrine of Original Sin proposed to free and candid examination* (1740), quoted in *The Hibbert Journal* (January 1963), p. 90. At last, as if to make up for centuries of metaphysical repression, we now have a Creation Centred Spirituality. See especially Matthew Fox, *Original Blessing* (New Mexico, Bear and Co, 1983).

II The Reintegration of Values

1. A. Koestler, *The Yogi and the Commissar* (London; Hutchinson, 1945).

2. C. Ponting, 'Politics or Real Change?' in *Resurgence* no. 127 (April, 1988) pp. 14–16.

3. E.P. Thompson, *The Heavy Dancers* (London; Merlin Press, 1985) pp. 2ff. Originally broadcast on Channel 4 'Opinion' (1982).

4. S.H. Nasr, *Knowledge and the Sacred* (Edinburgh, Edinburgh University Press, 1982). See especially chapter on 'Time and Eternity'.

5. D. Hay and A. Morisy, 'Reports on Ecstatic, Paranormal or Religious Experience in Great Britain and the US', *JSSR*, xvii, 1978. See also A. Hardy, *The Spiritual Nature of Man* (Oxford University Press, 1980).

6. B. Spinoza, *Tractatus Politicus* (Wernham ed.) p. 311.

7. B. Russell, *The History of Western Philosophy* (London; Allen and Unwin, 1946) p. 552.

8. J. Rowan, *Psychologists for Peace Newsletter* (Winter 1986).

9. A. Wetherall (ed) *The Mystical Experience of Loss of Freedom* (Scientific and Medical Network, 1987).

10. T. Merton, *Message to Poets* (Mexico, 1964) reprinted in *Raids on the Unspeakable* (London; Burns and Oates, 1977), p. 123.

III Sustainable Religion

1. W. Pelletier, 'Time', *Who is the Chairman of this Meeting?* (1972).

2. C.G. Jung, *Synchronicity – An Acausal Connecting Principle* (London; RKP, 1955).

3. A. Koestler, *Kaleidoscope* (London; Hutchinson, 1981).

4. P. Arrupe, *A Planet to Heal* (Rome, 1975), p. 26.

5. J. Garrison, *The Darkness of God: Theology after Hiroshima* (London; SCM Press, 1982) p. 70.

6. F. Capra, *The Turning Point* (London; Fontana, 1982) pp. 400ff.

7. T. Blackwell and J. Seabrook, *The Politics of Hope* (London; Faber, 1988) p. 111.

8. W. Schwarz, 'Face to Faith', *The Guardian,* 5 December 1988.

9. C. Spretnak and F. Capra, *Green Politics* (London; Paladin, 1985) p. 234.

10. L. Feuerbach, *Thoughts on Death and Immortality* (University of California Press, 1980) ed. Massey, p. ix.

11. E. Kamenka, *The Philosophy of Ludwig Feuerbach* (London, 1970).

12. Quoted in Kamenka, ibid., p. 10.

13. L. Feuerbach (Massey ed.) *op. cit.*

14. *Ibid.*, pp. 42–3.

15. J. Krishnamurti and D. Bohm, *The Ending of Time* (London; Gollancz, 1985).

16. J. Krishnamurti, *You are the World* (New York; Harper & Row, 1972) p. 135.

17. J. Krishnamurti, *Truth and Actuality* (London; Gollancz, 1977) p. 155.
18. T. Merton *Conjectures of a Guilty Bystander* (New York; Doubleday, 1964).

IV A Living Philosophy

1. H.H. Price, *Proceedings of the SPR,* 164, xlvi, (June, 1941) p. 271.
2. *Creative Evolution* (London; Macmillan, 1964) p. 252.
3. T.A. Goudge (ed) in Preface to *An Introduction to Metaphysics* (New York; Bobbs–Merrill, 1955) p. 9.
4. *Time and Free Will* (London; Allen & Unwin, 1910) p. 181.
5. *Ibid.*, p. 128.
6. *Ibid.*, p. 183.
7. *Matter and Memory* (London; Allen & Unwin, 1910) p. 70.
8. *The Doors of Perception* (London; Penguin, 1959).
9. *Mind Energy* (*l'Energie Spirituelle*, Lectures and Essays, 1920) p. 47.
10. *Proc. SPR*, xxvii, pp. 172–3.
11. *The Living Stream* (London; Collins, 1965) p. 253.
12. *The Divine Flame* (London; Collins, 1966) p. 27.
13. *Creative Evolution, op. cit.*, p. 116.
14. *Brain and Mind*, ed. J.R. Smythies (London; Routledge, 1965) p. 55.
15. Goudge, *op. cit.*, p. 15.
16. *Mind Energy, op. cit.*, p. 13.
17. *Ibid.*, pp. 1–2.
18. *Ibid.*, p. 28.
19. *The Varieties of Religious Experience* (London; Mentor, 1958) p. 298.
20. *The Two Sources of Morality and Religion* (New York; Doubleday, 1935) p. 53.
21. *Ibid.*

Appendix: Global Thinking

1. DE–CIDE, from Latin *de-cidere*, to cut apart.
2. Godel's Proof (1929) showed that any system of logic can be either consistent or complete, but not both.
3. See Erwin Schrodinger, *What is Life?* (1967), Fritjof Capra, *The Tao of Physics* (1975), Willis W. Harman, *An Incomplete Guide to the Future* (1979), and Willis Harman and Howard Rheingold, *Higher Creativity* (1984).